THE AWESOME GUIDE TO LIFE

itbooks
AN IMPRINT OF HARPERCOLLINS*PUBLISHERS*

THE *Awesome* GUIDE TO LIFE

GET FIT, GET LAID, GET YOUR SH*T TOGETHER

JASON ELLIS

WITH MIKE TULLY

HarperCollins books may be purchased for educational, business, or sales promotional use. For information please e-mail the Special Markets Department at SPsales@harpercollins.com.

FIRST EDITION

Designed by Shannon Plunkett

Library of Congress Cataloging-in-Publication Data

Ellis, Jason, 1971-

    The Awesome Guide to Life: get fit, get laid, get your sh*t together / Jason Ellis.

       pages cm

      ISBN 978-0-06-227015-3 (pbk.)—ISBN 978-0-06-227016-0 (ebook) 1. Ellis, Jason, 1971- 2. Ellis, Jason, 1971—Philosophy. 3. Skateboarders—United States—Biography. 4. Radio personalities—United States—Biography. 5. Martial artists—United States—Biography. I. Title.

      GV859.813.E56A3 2014

      796.22092—dc23

      [B]   2013029698

---

14 15 16 17 18   OV/RRD   10 9 8 7 6 5 4 3 2 1

AUTHOR'S NOTE

Anyone who is about to read this book should proceed at their own risk. I am not a doctor, a psychiatrist, a nutritionist, a marriage counselor, or anything like that. I have had no professional training of any kind. In fact, many people who have heard my radio show would consider me a dangerous moron.

All I have to offer is the knowledge that I am awesome, and the belief that I can help you become awesome, too.

But don't take it from me. Take it from my lawyers, who told me to tell you that "This book is written as a source of information only. The information contained in this book is based solely on my personal experience and observations of others and should by no means be considered a substitute for the advice, decision, or judgment of the reader's physician or other professional adviser. My publisher and I expressly disclaim responsibility for any adverse effects arising from the use or application of the information contained herein."

Consider yourself warned.

CONTENTS

THE AWESOME GUIDE TO LIFE

INTRODUCTION

IF YOU BOUGHT THIS BOOK, then I probably don't need to explain who I am or why I believe I am so ridiculously awesome.

But just in case, here's some background: After a twenty-year career in action sports, I retired as the seventh-greatest skateboarder in the world. Skaters don't actually have official rankings, but the last thing I entered was the Mega Ramp contest at the 2005 X Games. I finished seventh, so to me, that means I walked away as the seventh-best dude in the world. (Mind you, not everyone in skateboarding would agree with this opinion.)

Immediately after I retired, I started one of the biggest, most popular shows on satellite radio. And now, for the twenty hours a week I'm on the air, I get to talk about whatever the fuck I feel like talking about and do whatever the fuck I feel like doing. Once or twice a year, I throw an event called Ellismania in Las Vegas. On a Friday afternoon, I host my radio show poolside in front of a thousand fans. That night, I sing in front of those same thousand people with my band, Death! Death! Die! And then the next night I beat the shit out of a pro fighter in front of another sold-out crowd.

Also, when I'm not busy working, my bisexual nymphomaniac girlfriend arranges threesomes for me.

Not convinced that I am as awesome as I like to think I am? Then let me tell you some of the things I'm lucky enough to enjoy just because I'm me. When I go to the UFC, Dana White gives me tickets and I sit in the same row as the singer of the Red Hot Chili Peppers. I get direct messages on Twitter from Slash. Rob Flynn from Machine Head gives me a shout-out onstage when I go to see his band. When I go to Supercross, I can go anywhere I want and all the riders there know me. I can go to MMA gyms for free and get beaten up by legendary fighters like Dan Henderson and Babalu Sobral. I have been getting paid to wear clothing since I was sixteen years old. I have signature sunglasses. I have a signature shoe. I have my own hats and T-shirts and beanies and key chains. I get free crickets for my pet lizard, Supercross the Dragon. I have a signature guitar, and I can't even really play guitar.

But maybe that still isn't enough for you. Maybe you're still wondering, what is so fucking special about this egotistical moron named Jason Ellis? Why should I want to base my entire approach to life on what he's about to tell me?

Well, here's what my day has been known to consist of:

First and foremost, blow jobs. I frequently wake up with the mouth of an attractive lady already attached to my groin area. Sometimes there are two ladies in bed with me. When one of them wakes up and starts getting into it, usually that rocks the bed a bit and wakes the other one up. Then I often have two attractive ladies competing for my penis. I find that's an empowering way to start my day.

Next I hop in the shower. On a good day, the lady or ladies I spent the night with will team up to wash me. I get to relax while the girls clean my undercarriage. After that, I have been known to enjoy a bathtub foot job. I'm not actually a foot fetish guy. More often than not, bathtub foot jobs start out as a joke. But, like any man, I don't care what object you are using to massage my penis—there's only so long before shit turns serious.

Once I get out of the shower, I like to put on fluffy baby-blanket clothes. I like comfy shit. I also wear these skintight cheetah pants a lot around the house. In a perfect world, I would wear cheetah pants outside more often. But unfortunately, the world can't handle my extremely manly bulge. So I usually just have those on behind closed doors. After I get dressed, somebody might paint my nails for me, and then I usually play some video games and relax while somebody makes me breakfast.

Then I get in my car, which is a turbo Porsche. The first thing I think, every day, is, "I can't believe I own this car." I turn on some music. It's a pretty safe bet that it will be either AC/DC, Metallica, or Pantera. At that point, I usually open my sunroof, stick my hand out to feel the wind, and think, "Yeah me."

I drive my car stupidly fast. There is insane traffic in L.A., and I solve that problem as best I can by weaving around a lot. I like to cut through corners at gas stations so I can get ahead of all the fucktards in front of me, trying to slow me down. Because I have shit to do.

I definitely should try to stop driving like an idiot. I know it's bad. I mean, I haven't killed anybody yet. I don't cut people off and ram them into guardrails. But I'm not a fucking angel. I'm a dude. I enjoy driving, and I enjoy handling the steering wheel. I don't always set out to speed, but if you give me half an hour on the road, you will usually find me doing something stupid.

There are a couple different things I like to do before I go to work. I might head to the moto track and ride my dirt bike. If you have never ridden moto before, let me explain the sensation: riding moto is as close as a human can get to having robot powers. I'm nowhere near pro level, but if you have a decent bike, it becomes a part of you. You don't feel the weight of it anymore. I've jumped a hundred and twenty feet into the air on a bike. I can just be chilling and fucking around and still do like seventy-five feet. It's like being a shitty Iron Man.

In the summertime, instead of riding moto in the morning I might go to the ocean and do some stand-up paddleboarding or some surfing. I also like to ride my Jet Ski. I live in a city, but I like knowing that at any time I can drive down to the marina and get five miles away from any other human on the planet. On a Jet Ski, you can go out into the middle of the ocean, get completely naked, and just lie there. You can do anything and it doesn't matter, because if anybody was coming you could see them from miles away. You can relax and float around, and since you're on the Jet Ski, you know that sharks can't eat you.

Sharks freak me out. They are real-life monsters. Not some bullshit in a horror movie. Not some made-up Loch Ness monster. Sharks are remorseless killing machines. Hopefully I never have to face off against a shark. I've given the idea a lot of thought, and I may be a pretty tough guy, but I believe that's a bad matchup for me.

Speaking of fighting, sometimes in the morning I go to a gym to do some boxing or MMA. I love learning a new hand combo or doing some sparring. I've knocked people out before I've gone to work. And I don't spar with anyone who hasn't had pro fights. Sometimes the guys I spar with are twice my size. Which means I've gotten knocked out before work, too. To me, that is just as awesome. The better and the more famous the guy is, the more of a highlight it is for me to get punched by him. A busted face makes me really happy. If somebody gets me good and my eye is swelled up for a whole radio show, I'm super hyped about that. To me, black eyes are man makeup.

Going to the gym makes me tougher. It makes me look better, and that makes chicks want to fuck me. But most importantly, it lets me work out my man rage. I think a lot of men have a rage inside them that naturally comes with having testicles. But they don't know where to put it. Men have an instinctive need to battle, but there's no way to work that out in normal pussy society. I definitely do not suggest getting into street fights. I suggest going to the gym, facing another man, and then punching each other in the face. It's euphoric. It makes you feel alive. And, unlike street fights, at the end of the day you get to go home, instead of going to prison.

If there's time in the morning I also go to the spa. I like to sit in the steam room and visualize taking over the world. I use visualization a lot. It's like meditation, only it's the exact opposite. Meditation is thinking about nothing. But when I visualize, I'm thinking about everything. My brain's going a thousand miles an hour, trying to solve all the puzzles in front of me—what I've got to do today, this week, this month, this year, and so on. I'm laying out all the events that need to happen for me to become the ultimate overlord of everything.

And then I get a mud mask—with the cucumbers on my eyes and everything—followed by a mango smoothie. To a stranger, a guy like me in a mud mask probably looks like a very fruity murderer. But I believe that to get the most out of life, sometimes you have to be willing to look a little fruity.

When you go to the spa, you get some alone time. That might be the best part of it. You also sweat and get shit out of your system. If I'm sore from all the other stuff I've been doing, the spa will fix me up. When you leave, it feels like they put new blood inside you.

Once I'm done at the spa, I take a shower and get ready for work. I shave my head and my beard. Everything has to be tight. I put my chains on. Then I put on my slippers. They have golden spikes all over them, which makes them very metal, as far as slippers go. I like looking at my metal feet. It makes me feel good about my toes.

Everything I wear is synchronized with everything else. But not in obvious ways. Anybody can wear a blue hat and a blue sweater. If the way your stuff matches is too over-the-top, then to me that's corny. I like to go for the undercover color coordination. I like running a tight ship. There aren't many people who are going to notice. It's very rare that someone says, "Pardon me, but do your shoelaces match the fucking lining of your boxers?" But when people do notice things like that, then I know they must be running a very tight ship themselves. There's a whole secret society of us out there, noticing each other's tight ships. It's obviously also a secret society of fucking assholes, because holy shit, who cares about this crap? But I'm not going to lie—when I know I've got my beanie and my underwear and my socks all working together in harmony, it's pretty hard to ruin my day.

Then I'm off to the radio studio. Even with all the other ways I spend my time, when the show is firing off at peak level, that right there is the highlight of my day. Sometimes really famous people come by and say really flattering stuff to me. I once set the satellite radio record for the most phone calls in one hour. Hot chicks get naked a lot in the studio, too. It's pretty cool to be at work and get to meet super-hot chicks who think I'm sexy and want to bang me. And yes, I may or may not have done a couple of porn chicks from the show.

But that's not the best part of being on the radio. The best part is getting to be myself in front of a huge audience of listeners. I don't think too many other people who are on the radio get the same thing out of it that I do. If you're an FM cheese dick, then you're really just reading from a script. You're playing the part of wacky radio dude. But I get to tell the whole world everything I really think and everything I've ever done. Radio is like my therapist, but it's bigger than that, because other people are listening to my story. I think I am a somewhat insane person, but the more I talk on the radio, the more I cure myself of being insane.

Mind you, I was doing the same thing before radio came along. I was talking to a wall or to the back of some drunk dude's head. The only difference is, now I figured out a way to get paid for it.

My success on the radio is a massive big deal to me. It's an accomplishment that makes people acknowledge me and respect me. People from the moto world and the MMA world know me because of the show, and that's a dream come true. I don't think big-time people give you the time of day unless you've done something. It's just the way of the world. It doesn't hurt that I'm also the skateboarder guy who punches people in the face, but the radio show has taken me to another level.

Because I'm on the radio, I get to ask famous people questions that normal people wouldn't be allowed to ask. If you're a fan of Slash, and you ran into him at the airport or something, you wouldn't get to ask him how much sex he's had on private jets. He would tell you to fuck off. But because I have a radio show, I can tell you that Slash has licked Bacardi 151 from a girl's vagina at thirty thousand feet.

All that stuff is great. But most of all, I believe that, on a good day, me and the people on my show are funnier than anyone's ever been in the history of radio. And when one of those days happens, I drive home with that feeling in my belly, and it keeps me warm. That's what it's really all about.

After the show, I might go record some music with my band or hang out with my bestie, Benji Madden. Or the pool at my house might be heated up with girls there waiting for me. I keep waterproof lube stashed in a plant at poolside, so I'm ready to go at all times.

If you're going to have sex in a pool, you definitely need to have underwater lube. And you still can't do it too often, because you end up smashing a bunch of water inside of your chick, and you can't ask her to put up with that every day. But if you do it right and you have the right lube, then you can fuck somebody while both of you are basically weightless. When a woman is floating, you can do all kinds of things to her that you didn't think were humanly possible.

My sex life is all about pushing the limits. I know a lot of people reading this book will wonder why I need to go so far. I don't think garden-variety sex is bad, if that's what you're into. And I know from experience that some people are like that, and they're very content. But personally, I want to try to do as many things as I can before I die, and that's especially true when it comes to sex. I'm up for anything I haven't tried.

Not that long ago, my girlfriend arranged for a girl to stay at my house for a few days as a sex slave. She had to do whatever me and my chick wanted. It actually wasn't as great as it sounds. It turns out I'm not that creative when it comes to slave driving. But it was nice being able to think of a bunch of different threesome positions and then snap my fingers and make them all come true.

I've never had more in common with a chick than I do with my girlfriend. We're both humongous show-offs. We're both really white trash. Redneck things make us feel at home. We live in Ugg boots and pajamas and eat bacon and listen to metal. Also, we're better at sex than anybody else I've ever seen, on TV or in real life. I've had sex with porn stars who have won awards. We might not be as hot as them, but we are the champions of fucking.

My girlfriend is a sex expert who is constantly trying to reinvent the game. She's also probably the horniest person I've ever met. Recently, she stuck a vibrator up my butt and blew me at the same time, and I literally had multiple orgasms. She had spent a bunch of money on the thing, and she really wanted to stick it in me. I told her if it made her happy then she could go for it.

I started to come, and naturally I was expecting the load to come out. But then it didn't. The feeling came and went, and then it started all over again. It took me a second to realize—*Dude, you're having a chick orgasm! You are officially multiorgasmic!*

Afterward, my girlfriend asked me how many times I came, and I wasn't sure. I always thought it was weird when you asked chicks that question after an extended jam session and they couldn't answer for sure. No matter how many times I have come in an evening, at the end of it, I have always been able to pinpoint an exact number. But now I knew how they felt. It was maybe four or five times in a row? I'm not really sure. I'm forty-one, and before that night, that had never happened to me, ever.

I don't care if you know that things have gone up my butt. That doesn't bother me. I don't care if you think I'm gay. Fuck everybody. That was amazing.

After a night like that, I go to bed happy. And then I wake up the next day and do it all over again.

I'm not saying all of this stuff happens to me every day. But I'm not making anything up here. This is how I live on a daily basis. Well, unless I have the kids that day. Then, forget just about everything I just said.

If you don't want this life I lead, then this probably isn't the book for you. But maybe you also want to have sex with multiple partners and then talk about it on the radio while wearing cheetah pants. Or maybe you have some goals of your own that you need help pursuing. Whatever the case may be, I believe that I possess every single piece of information you need to make your dreams come true.

I don't think I'm the most gifted person in the world. I don't think I'm untalented, but starting from birth, I probably had about the same chances that you did. I'm just very driven. I try extremely hard at all the things that I do.

I see so many people who never try anything at all. They don't try to pursue their dreams. They don't try at their jobs. They don't even try in their marriages. There are so many people who go through life at 80 percent. I'm not saying you have to go 110 percent all the time. I do, and I constantly wear myself out. But with this book, I feel like I can motivate people to try harder and become better.

The world offers you millions of things to get into, and if you're not falling passionately and maniacally in love with at least one of them, then to me, you're wasting your life. I feel like some people figure that out, and then they step it up, and it makes their lives better. They become more successful. They get treated better by other people. They live longer, and they're happier. I'm not saying everybody needs to be fucking Ryan Seacrest and work all the time and sleep one hour a day. But I think everybody wants to have some kind of success. And I think everybody can have it, if they go after it the right way.

And it's not just about work. It's about getting off your ass and maximizing all the opportunities that life has to offer. It's about not being a pussy. It's about remembering that you are alive, right now, and that won't always be the case. So do something. Anything. Enjoy the ride. Go outside and get naked. Let your genitals see the sunshine. Enjoy your penis, and let Mother Nature enjoy your penis. What do you have to lose?

By reading this book, you can learn from my mistakes. I've made plenty of them. I can tell you why you don't want to rush into getting married and why you should not let two random street hookers inject heroin into your arm.

You can learn from my successes. I can show you that if you pour ten years of determination into doing something you love, you will reap the benefits. I did it with skateboarding, and I'm doing it now on the radio. It doesn't matter what you want to be great at. Get awesome at bowling. See if I care.

If you are a dude reading this book, I can tell you how to handle pretty much every situation life is going to throw at you and how to play it like a champ. I can tell you how to look, how to act, how to pick up a stripper—you name it.

If you're a woman, this book will give a brutally honest view into how men think about you. It will probably change the way you think of us—and in some ways maybe for the better.

Depending on how old you are and how much you've lived, you may not need help with all the topics we're about to cover. But there's no man (or woman) alive who can't learn something from what I have to say.

And it all starts as soon as you turn this page.

HOW TO GET FIT

IS IT EASIER FOR ME to impress people and meet girls now that I have some money and some jewelry and a Porsche? Of course. Does it help that I have a radio show airing all across America and Canada, and that hot bitches can occasionally see me on MTV and then find me on Twitter? Sure. (By the way, if any hot bitches are reading this right now, my Twitter is @ellismate. Don't be shy, ladies.) Things may be a little less difficult for me nowadays. But I haven't always been awesome.

If you're a young guy just starting out in the game, know that I was once just like you. I started off as a poor, lame skate rat from Sandringham, a small town outside Melbourne, Australia. I don't think I was born special at all. And life did not do me any favors. I sincerely believe that I possess no special skills, other than the drive to work as hard as possible to get everything I want.

I also believe that if I can do it, then so can you.

If you're okay with sucking, then suck away. Be my guest. But deep down, I don't think anybody really feels that way. And I don't believe that anyone is destined to be a loser.

The only people who are truly hopeless are people who believe they're hopeless. And I know how people start to think that way. Kids say a bunch of mean shit to you in school. And either your parents are too stupid to see what's going on or they don't give enough of a shit to help you out. Insecurities start creeping in when you're little, and then you start building up walls to cover those insecurities. At some point, you have so many walls built up, you decide you'd rather go down with the ship than admit your faults and try to fix yourself.

Throughout this book, I'll be giving you a bunch of tips on how to come across a little bit cooler. But over and over I'm also going to tell you that being awesome really comes down to having confidence. When people are insecure, they will find a way to fuck themselves over, no matter what the situation. To get what you really want out of life, you first have to be comfortable in your own skin. True confidence isn't something most people are born with. It's something they have to earn. In this chapter, you will learn how to develop the positive attitude that will allow you to truly make things happen.

I think it's extremely hard to have confidence if you don't like the way you look. Getting in shape makes you look better, and getting more fit is something that's within reach for most people. So let's start there.

If you are currently a fat useless piece of shit, the first thing you need to do is to change your attitude. You need to develop the discipline to wake up with the same positive mind-set every morning. If you are unfit, that means you eat shitty food and you don't work out enough. So you're going to have to change your diet and exercise more, and you will need to be consistent with both of those. As your body transforms, the confidence that gives you will be something you can then build off of.

I truly believe that your attitude is your decision. You are what you say you are. Take willpower, for example. If you come to the conclusion that you lack willpower, then I guarantee you'll be right. Because, just like confidence, willpower isn't something you're born with—it's a decision. It's something you find inside yourself when you decide you need something bad enough.

Of course, some people are legitimately depressed. If you can't get happy, even though there's no reason for you to be sad, then you've got to talk to somebody. If the sensible adult part of your brain knows that what's bumming you out really shouldn't be that big of a deal, then you need to go see a therapist.

But I don't think that applies to most miserable people. A lot of miserable people are just hell-bent on being miserable for the rest of their days. Some people are happy being sad. I don't know why. If you're down in the dumps all the time, girls don't want to hear about it, especially if you just met them. And your friends can only take so much negativity before they decide to get rid of you. If your friends are healthy and happy and you're not, eventually they won't be your friends anymore. They'll disappear, because nobody wants to be around that. It's contagious.

And that goes both ways. If your friends are all a bunch of depressed losers, it's going to be hard to not get caught up in their loser stink. It's just like when you hang out with a bunch of people who smoke cigarettes. It's only a matter of time before you light up, too. We're all sheep. That goes for me, too. Your friends rub off on you, for better and for worse. So ask yourself who your top five friends are. If more than one of them is unemployed, a drug dealer, or a psychopath, then you might want to add some new friends to the mix.

I'll say it again: You attitude is your decision. If you were in a bad mood and somebody offered you a million dollars to cheer up, would you do it? Of course you would.

What's so bad about being fat? Well, it's scientifically proven that being fat makes you stupider. It's like the fat chokes off the blood to your brain or something. (I don't know how it works exactly, but you can look it up.) Maybe that's why fat people don't realize they're dying. Maybe the fat seeps into their brain and makes them give up.

I think we can all agree that any fat person can lose some weight if they put their mind to it. So why would you not give it a go? You only live once. Skinnier people get treated better than fat people do. Life is kinder to them. That's the way it is. We all know this.

If you're not born fat but you just let yourself go, I think that's even worse. If you're fat from the get-go, I think maybe you come to terms with it, and you can be happy like that. But when you're young and fit, and then you put on weight, it's almost like you're already giving in to death. As you're getting bigger, you're letting yourself deteriorate. You're letting yourself get old. Psychologically, that takes a toll. I don't understand why you would go along with that.

I also don't understand people who are always ten pounds over-weight and stay that way for their whole life. You've got to get super fit, at least one time. It just has to be done. If you get yourself in great shape once, I bet you that experience will inspire you to want to stay like that. Have you ever looked at a girl who is super hot, only she's a little bit chunky? And then you think, "Man, if only she lost a little bit of weight . . ." Right? Well, guess what: They think the same thing about us.

I see pretty girls who are fifteen pounds overweight and who stay that way forever. And I think a girl like that is really missing out. There's a solid twenty-year period where she could be meeting people and traveling and living a completely different life with a different body. Fifteen pounds is not that hard to lose, and if she pulls it off, she will be treated in a completely different way for the rest of her life. We can all bitch and moan about how that shouldn't be the case. But we all know it's true.

And not being fat isn't just about the way other people look at you or the way they treat you. If you're overweight, you're missing out on all kinds of stuff. For starters, there are all the physical things you can't do with your body. And more importantly, I feel like fat people hide. You develop this shame thing, and that in turn makes you eat more.

On the other hand, if you're fit, you enjoy showing yourself off. You get up in the morning and just seeing yourself makes you happy. Just looking in the mirror becomes the greatest pep talk you could ever give yourself. You won't know it until you try it, but when you look in the mirror and you see what you can accomplish, it will change the way you feel about food. Food is cool, but that feeling is way better.

And believe me, I love to eat as much as the next guy. Maybe even more than the next guy. I've had people try to tell me, "Oh, I just have a different body type than you." Bullshit you do. I'm not a different body type. I'm a fat guy waiting to happen, the same as everybody else. If I don't go to the gym and I sit on the couch eating pizza for a year, I will be a fucking 250-pound man. I just try to stay on top of it. Even when I don't have time to really train, I still do stuff that I don't think average people do in the morning. If I can't get to the gym, then maybe three days a week, I'll still do at least some kind of exercise for half an hour. And even if I do throw myself a one-man pizza party, it's only for like a day. I don't go off the rails permanently.

I think most guys don't know anything about food and nutrition, which is crazy, because you're supposed to be an adult. Almost every aspect of the typical shithead dude diet is dead wrong. Luckily, it isn't that hard or expensive to fix it, if you're willing to completely change the way you eat.

If you want to seriously change your diet, then obviously fast food is out the window. You can't drink soda. You can't eat a bunch of cheese or pie or cake. You can't drink too much alcohol. And you definitely can't smoke. To me, smoking is the most insane thing any human can do. It makes me think a lot less of people. If I had to choose between dating someone who smokes every day and someone who snorts a little heroin every Saturday night, then sign me up for the part-time junkie.

I don't recommend any crazy diets. Don't commit yourself to anything where you only eat cheese, or you only eat lettuce, or whatever. Juicing is cool, but you still need to eat actual food at some point. You should eat plenty of vegetables. Don't eat too much meat, and don't eat shitty meat. Don't eat white bread. If I have bread at all, I have wheat bread, and I only have it one time a day. If you're going to eat spaghetti, I would have whole wheat pasta.

You should eat four small meals a day. That keeps your metabolism up. But it's all about portions. Even if you're eating healthy food, you shouldn't eat a humongous bowl of anything. I wouldn't even eat a humongous bowl of salad. You probably can't carry a measuring cup with you everywhere you go, but as a rule of thumb, when you have a meal, you want to eat a protein—steak, or chicken, or fish—that's the size of the palm of your hand, and then two palmfuls of veggies or carbs. If you do that all the time, then I guarantee you will not be fat.

If you're a bachelor dude starting out on your own, you can't just live off takeout and microwave food and all that processed garbage. Your mommy doesn't take care of you anymore. Cooking stuff is not that difficult. You don't need to become a chef or anything. You just need to figure out some basics.

Breakfast is easy. You can't afford to eat out three meals a day anyway, unless you're rich, so you've got to make breakfast at home. And besides, if you're serious about being in shape, then eating out all the time is stupid.

You shouldn't be anywhere near a fast-food place for breakfast, unless it's every now and again, because you're hungover. In that case, I will allow the occasional McMuffin. But in general, organic oatmeal isn't hard to find, and it's super good for you. It's instant, so you can't fuck it up. (Actually, come to think of it, my ex-wife used to fuck up oatmeal. I did not marry her for her cooking.) Don't get flavored oatmeal, because that has sugar in it. Although you can add protein powder. Protein powder has sugar in it, but that isn't really cheating. So if you want something sweet, go for that.

You can also eat Ezekiel cereal with almond milk. Most cereals in the store are just a bunch of processed sugar and bullshit. Ezekiel cereal is the real deal. It may not come with a toy inside, but if you're able to read this book, then it's time for you to start eating legitimate adult food. (If your local store doesn't have Ezekiel stuff, you can find it online.) And any idiot should be able to cook an egg and turkey bacon and make toast. Wash any of the foods I've just mentioned down with orange juice, and black coffee, if you want it.

Healthy lunches are also easy. Salads are kind of fruity, I will admit. But if you can make them, you just have to get one of those little plastic tub things, and then you can put everything in there and shake it up. Just don't use too much dressing or else you might as well be going to KFC.

Sandwiches are even easier. And you can live off them forever, because you can always change up what's inside. I'm a Neanderthal and I can't really cook, so I just keep making different sandwiches. I live off those fuckers. Just make sure you put healthy stuff in the middle. Don't use shitty meat. Don't buy any of that fake shitty cheese. Don't use white bread. Don't use butter. You can get stuff that's just like butter that doesn't have dairy in it, and it doesn't taste any different when you mix it in with the other stuff on a sandwich.

If you're looking for a snack, I would avoid any of those energy bars. That's just a Snickers with some protein in it. It's not good for you. If you're younger, you can get away with it because you'll burn it off, but otherwise that isn't going work. I'm not even sure I believe they have as much protein as they say they do. There's one that supposedly has sixty grams of protein, but that's because it's about ten inches long. If you eat that, you've just had like seven Snickers bars. So congratulations on your diet.

For snacks, I would just leave my house with apples and pears. Get little individual packets of almond butter. Or look into those little fruit bars they have at health food stores. That one will probably take a little trial and error. That's the problem with vegan, healthy, gluten-free food—half of it tastes like shit. If you find a bar that is worth swallowing, just stick to it, because trust me, you're probably not going to find another one.

Nuts are the easiest snack of all. You can buy them at the fucking supermarket. And even if you are the most useless turd imaginable, you can keep them in the pantry and then pull them out and grab a handful whenever you're hungry. You never have to starve. You have to keep eating all the time. That raises your metabolism and makes you less of a fat person.

For dinner, you have your one lean protein, the size of the palm of your hand, and your veggies or carbs the size of two of your palms.

There. That is everything you need to know about food.

Next up is exercise. I believe you need to find something that motivates you to keep exercising, or sooner or later you're going to quit. If you're trying to lose weight, then just seeing the pounds come off can sometimes be enough. Personally, I am inspired by my insecurity. I am a man who was born with baby shoulders, and I either go to the gym every day and then get to look in the mirror and smile every now and again, or else I live in a world of anguish and hell. Those are my only two options.

If you are really out of shape, you need to start with the absolute basics, and that would be stretching. If you're super unfit, your muscles won't be ready for anything that you do. And then you'll be in pain after you work out, and that pain might deter you from ever going back to the gym. So I would focus on stretching.

If you don't know what kind of exercise you want to get into, I would start with running. Everybody knows how to do that. If you're really fat, running is going to fuck your ankles up, so in that case at first I would do the StairMaster or a bike. If you're really, really big, then at first you should probably just walk. You've got to walk before you can run, or whatever that bullshit is.

If you can afford a gym membership, I think lifting weights is cool. But if you're going to lift weights, you absolutely have to pay the kook in the gym shirt to teach you how to do it right. The guys at your local gym might not be the best, but they're way smarter than you are. If you think you can go in there and just start throwing weights around, you are wrong. You'll be wasting your money, and you will not see the results you want.

If running on a treadmill for hours at a time makes you happy, then I say go with it. But personally, that would drive me insane. When I look at people running on treadmills, I usually just see a bunch of angry people who are punishing themselves for being fat. There are definitely some chicks who love nothing more than getting on a treadmill, pumping Lady Gaga into their headphones, and pounding it out. But if that's not you, eventually treadmills will break your will.

If you get bored with your gym routine—which is probably what will happen to most people—then try to find something else you can get really into. For me, the best thing I've come across is training in MMA. Even if you have no intention of having an MMA fight, just going to the gym and learning new techniques every day can become addictive. Plus, girls love guys who train in MMA. If you want to get laid quick, the most direct route is to become a fighter. All chicks dig fighters, whether or not they realize it or want to admit it. Girls want someone who can fight and protect them and open jars of mayonnaise. They get off on it. All of them.

There is a certain level of dedication to fighting that might turn some girls off. If you have cauliflower ear or if your face is chewed up, that might be a problem. If you smell like a staph infection, you're probably overdoing it. And being a fighter isn't going to be enough to impress all the girls, all by itself. But if you have some muscles and some fighting skills, I promise you that doesn't hurt your chances with anyone.

But MMA is just one option. Anything that gets you off your ass and moving around can only be a good thing. If you're one of those people who have to spend the whole day working for the man, it's especially important to get a hobby. You need an outlet. You need a passion. Watching TV doesn't count. Nowadays, everyone— including me—spends way too much time staring at the TV and staring at their phone. As far as I'm concerned, every single second you spend watching TV, playing video games, and looking at your phone is wasted time. (Unless you're playing with your phone while you're taking a shit. I consider that multitasking.)

If you don't care about your job and you're just doing something to pay the bills and maybe support a family, eventually the job becomes mindless. And when your body figures out that it's only being used for mindless activity, that's when it gets easy to give up. It gets easy to start eating the wrong stuff all the time or start abusing yourself in other ways. It's a dangerous path, and once you start going in that direction, you can get stuck there permanently. If your life isn't physically challenging, then I believe you have to create the challenge for yourself. You have to satisfy your inner caveman.

Obviously my first big physical passion was skateboarding. If anyone reading this book right now is fifteen years old, then I would encourage you to start skateboarding. (I would also encourage you to put this book down, because it's way too offensive for fifteen-year-olds.) But if you're a dude in your thirties and you want to start skating now, I would advise against it. You can get a longboard and go cruise a boardwalk somewhere, if you want. But if you get a short stick and you're in your midthirties, you are a raging moron. It's too late. You're going to break your arm.

And in case you haven't broken a bone since you were a kid, let me inform you that a broken bone at thirty-five isn't the same as a broken bone at fifteen. When you break a bone as a kid, you basically go into shock. But once you get older, breaking your arm isn't going to send you into shock. You're just going to feel the pain, and you're going to realize that broken bones really fucking hurt.

So if you're going to start skating at thirty-five, never try anything that involves lifting your front wheels off the ground. If you do, you're going to the hospital. As soon as you decide that you really want to put your trucks on the shiny bit at the top of the bowl, skateboarding has booby-trapped you, and you are a dead man.

If you're already an adult and you want to get outside and start doing some shit, in my opinion you're better off trying moto. If you want to get into moto, the most important thing is to start small. Sometimes at the track you'll see some dude trying to work out a midlife crisis on a brand-new 450 cc bike. That guy has no idea how ballsy he's being. Not only can a 450 easily do fifty miles per hour, it can also do it in about two seconds. Try throwing yourself into a dirt mound at fifty miles per hour. We are talking about some lung-collapsing g-forces.

If you're a beginner, you just want to get a 50 cc bike. Those do thirty miles per hour, tops. And then you want to start out in an open field. Your first time on a dirt bike, trust me, you don't want any turns or jumps. You should try to be somewhere that doesn't even have any trees. Because you're going to panic. Everybody does.

Every time I try to show somebody how to ride, I tell them that if they think they're going too fast, they should hit the foot brake, not the front brake on the handlebars. They all say, "Okay, I got it." And then they all hit the gas and tear off, and then they all panic. They aren't prepared for what the bike is able to do, and then their instincts kick in from riding a bicycle. They grab the front brake. And then the bike locks up and drops to the side, and then the dude rips his leg up. Beginner moto can get pretty gory.

I even tell people that if you're riding a 50 and it gets bad, you should just stand up and let the bike go. And then once again they tell me they've got it, and then they tear off, and then the next thing you know, they're on their side with a bike on top of them, and the tire is grinding on their leg.

But eventually you get it, and when you do, moto is glorious. You've got power and speed and jumps and engines and noise. It's a man's sport.

Luckily, if you are that madman with a midlife crisis and a 450, chances are you won't manage to kill yourself. If you don't know how to ride, you won't even make it around the track. And besides, if there are any good riders there, they're going to stop you. Good moto dudes respect people who ride, even kooks.

Which is more than I can say for surfers. People have this impression that surfers are a bunch of peace-loving hippies. But that couldn't be farther from the truth. Actually, in my experience surfers are some of the biggest assholes you will ever encounter. If you don't know how to surf, they take your wave with no remorse.

A part of me gets it. Usually the guys you're surfing with grew up on that beach. They've all been surfing there together since they were little kids. It's their wave. And you're just this fucking idiot with a shiny new board and some stupid wetsuit and that zinc sunblock shit all over your face, because you're not used to the sun like they all are.

Surfers will yell at you, out there on the water. "Fuck you, kook! Watch where you're going!" If that happens to you, I say stand up for yourself. Don't apologize. It's not your fault you don't know what you're doing. Tell that guy to fuck off. Surfers are cocksuckers. They only respect other cocksuckers.

But then you do need to back off a bit. As a surfer, you've got to pay your dues. You've got to let the guys who know what they're doing ride the good wave, and you have to go ride the shit wave until you start to figure it out. Luckily, with all the magazines and videos and the Internet, it's a lot easier to learn than it used to be.

It's hard getting into any new activity, but it's always worth it in the end. I think that's especially true when it comes to surfing, because it lets you spend time in the ocean. And you can learn things from the ocean. The ocean will make you humble. Because if you do become a surfing enthusiast, sooner or later—and probably sooner—you will be temporarily drowned. A wave will pull you under and chew you up, and that will remind you that you are a minuscule amoeba compared to the size of the ocean and the size of this planet.

Speaking of getting chewed up, if you are out in the waves all the time, you will never lose sight of the fact that you are swimming among sharks. I was always afraid that if I went surfing, a shark was gonna eat me. I think that's why I didn't start surfing until later in life. My whole life I've been afraid of sharks. But then I started thinking, *You know what? I go on the radio every day, and I tell people about conquering their fears and hardening the fuck up, so how can I not do this?* I've given this subject a lot of thought, and I can tell you that if I am to be eaten by a shark, when that monster is chewing me, that indeed will be a horrific experience. But I am a man. And a man stays cool. My shark battle plan is ready at all times.

Sharks come up on you from behind. And that means that if my day of reckoning should ever arrive, I will not see the shark coming. I will die, but not before I give the shark a couple of good shots. He may bite my leg off, but as he does that, he will be receiving one of my thumbs in his eyeball. I guarantee it. That's how I roll.

Assuming your day is shark-free, being in the ocean is pretty much the most peaceful thing there is. When you're a kid, you might not respect that. But when you get older, you are able to appreciate that the ocean is the last untouched thing there is. It's the only thing left on the planet that still looks the same as it did before mankind showed up and started taking a shit everywhere.

Whether or not you manage to catch a wave, getting up early in the morning and being out on the water is very therapeutic. You might spend the rest of the day being pissed off because your girlfriend left you, or because we're in a recession, or because someone said something fucked up to you on Facebook. But if you can start your day paddling out on the water, I find that helps you see the bigger picture.

Trying something out for the first time can be intimidating. But you need to get over that. If it's your first time at the gym, or it's your first day surfing, or whatever, and everybody can tell, who cares? Stick with it. It won't last forever. Embrace being a clueless tool bag.

It can be extremely challenging to keep up your diet, day after day, or to keep putting the hours in at the gym, or whatever you decide to do to stay in shape. It can be hard to maintain a positive attitude in general, no matter what you're trying to accomplish. Believe me, there are two people in my head, and one of them is not really a fan of me. I'm very critical of other people—especially on the radio—but the other me in my head is just as critical of every little thing that I do. When I slip, I beat myself up hard. I have to be very careful about saying negative stuff about myself, or even thinking it.

I remember the first time it happened. I was a skateboarder, and I was basically too good. I was a good-looking kid who was the best skateboarder in Australia by miles. There was one hot chick in skateboarding, and I was fucking her. I was the lucky guy.

But nobody likes a guy who's too perfect. I think that's particularly true in Australia. So I started trying to say stuff about how I sucked, so that I didn't seem too cool for people. With all the things I had going for me, I was afraid that everyone would assume I was a cocksucker. I tried to play myself down, so that normal guys would think I was cool.

And I really believe that was the beginning of me starting to say too much negative shit about myself. I think I told myself that too many times, and I picked up a weird negativity. I still fight with that, to this day.

One thing I find helpful for staying positive is saying mantras. Not just one time, here or there. You do it every day. When I wake up in the morning, I say stuff to myself. "Today is a great day." Not "It's going to be." It *is*.

I say it out loud. I don't care. I tell myself that I can do anything. I say, "My attitude is my decision." I'm not just telling you that in this book. I tell myself that all the time. When I feel weak or tired, that helps me. That alone can pick me up for half an hour. It's like a coffee.

Make no mistake—if you don't want to change and improve yourself, then you may well be doomed forever. It's a competitive world. And it's a materialistic world, too. There aren't enough good jobs and hot chicks to go around. Sad but true. Deal with it. I'm not saying that everybody can have it all. But if you think there's more to life than what you have right now, I'm here to tell you you're right. You just have to make an effort.

Let me remind everyone reading this book that Father Time is a humongous prick. I have hair on my back. I have hair on my ears. And I have no hair on my head. When I was seventeen, no one told me this was what I had to look forward to. Whatever you think is holding you back, my guess is it's not all that bad. If you can still grow a ponytail, then I don't want to hear any of your bitching.

2

HOW TO GET YOUR SHIT TIGHT

NOW THAT YOU'RE WORKING ON your attitude and getting your fat ass into shape, the next thing to think about is how you look. Some guys may still think it's lame or girly for a man to give a shit about style. But like it or not, the things that you wear say a lot about you. If you dress like a lumberjack, that's fine, but you're drastically limiting the number of women who might potentially sleep with you. If you look like a creepy loser all the time, no one's gonna make you stop. Just know that everyone who sees you is going to assume you're a creepy loser. That's just the way it is. It doesn't matter how great you are on the inside. If you look like a creepy loser, most people will never find that out, because they won't give you the time of day to begin with.

If you're a young guy who just jumped in the game and you're trying to figure out how to dress, here are some basics. First of all, you don't need to have logos stitched everywhere on your clothes. I know you're a dude and you think it's awesome to have a tiger embroidered on your shirt, but you're wrong. Also, if you don't get paid by Affliction, you shouldn't wear Affliction. Simple as that. In general, I don't think it's a good idea to wear any brand of fight T-shirts unless you're a professional fighter and someone is paying you to wear them.

And just in case you haven't gotten the memo, all dudes need to immediately stop wearing jeans that have giant crosses stitched across the ass pockets. At this point, I don't even think girls should be seen looking like that. If you're a Mexican dude and you wanna wear those kinds of jeans along with a shiny belt buckle and a cowboy hat, I'm backing that. But if you're a white dude and you still own any jeans that match this description, I would recommend that you put this book down and immediately set them on fire.

So what should you do? If you are a complete fashion moron, at first I would just try to keep it plain. If you jump in headfirst, you're going to wear something you'll regret. Just because you saw a celebrity wearing something in a magazine doesn't mean it's right for you. Don't believe the hype. If you try something on and you have even the slightest feeling it might not work for you, then trust your suck radar and don't risk it.

Avoid committing to anything drastic. I wouldn't put holes in my face unless I only wanted to have sex with people who also have holes in their faces. Make small adjustments. Try to figure out what kind of person you are, and what kind of person you are not.

Personally, I believe that I'm going to be a famous celebrity entertainer. And my look reflects the image that I want people to see. I look dangerous. I look evil. I look potentially angry. I also look like an athlete, because my skateboard style is hard to get rid of. In general, I look like someone that chicks want to fuck.

I look sweet. But if you try to look like me, you're probably going to look like a jackass.

If you're completely helpless, you should look for people who have a similar vibe to yours, and a similar complexion, and then try to copy them. Go for a mellow version of them until you start to get the hang of it. That's the key word here: "mellow."

I definitely wouldn't go trying to make any statements with my jeans. As we've already established, a bunch of stitching and patches on the ass are a no-no. But if you're wearing skinny-leg jeans, that's also making a statement. And if you've got baggy jeans, that's a statement, too. If you're just trying to hang, go find some slim-fit jeans. That's what your standard normal dude should be wearing these days. Unless you're forty-five and you're a dad and you're kind of out of shape. Then you can go a little baggy. No one wants to see middle-aged fat dads in slim-fit.

With jeans, you also don't want to get too creative with the color. Once again, if you don't know what you're doing, don't attract attention to yourself. From time to time, when I'm in "look at me" mode, I might bust out some white jeans. But you can't go wrong with black or blue.

When it comes to shoes, keep it basic. Just make sure they're clean and not worn out, and for the love of Christ, get your laces straightened out. I'm telling you, chicks care about that. Your laces need to be flat. They can't be all twisted up. And don't make them too tight, or else you'll look like a schoolteacher. Unless you're going running in those sneakers, there is no need to lace them up like Rambo. You shouldn't have to untie your shoes to take them off. You can tie them loose, and they're still not going to fall off. And don't make the loops too big. It shouldn't look like you have bunny ears on your feet.

Flip-flops are pretty sketchy to me, especially if they've got a bottle opener built into them. Flip-flops are okay at the beach. If you want to wear them at a barbecue, I would let that slide, too, although that's probably just because I'm Australian. But that's about it. In general, guys get way too happy on flip-flops.

Under no circumstances are sandals ever a good idea. Flip-flops tell me you've given up, but sandals tell me you never knew what was up in the first place. And by the way, if shell necklaces ever had a legitimate run, that run is now officially over. Sandals are the shell necklaces of footwear, and vice versa.

When it comes to underwear, you've got some options. Different girls like different things, and women are the only people you should be trying to impress with your undies. In my mind, the most important thing is ensuring proper testicle support. Boxers are fine, if that's how you want to roll. But if you're an active guy like me, the problem is that boxers don't hold anything. Back in the day, when I would wear boxers while I was skating, my nuts used to smack the inside of my leg. It felt like I was getting kicked in the dick all the time. So personally, the tighter they are, the more I like them.

I would never wear white underwear. Again, I'm thinking of the ladies here. If you're out at the club, and you meet some chick, and then you stay out all night dancing and drinking and maybe doing a couple bumps of cocaine, you never know—you could end up with some skid marks. And shit is not a good look. Pee stains alone are valid grounds for immediate dismissal by the ladies. So I wouldn't even go with red. Just stick with black.

Free-balling can be cool. Sometimes I might do it if the pants I'm wearing are tight and underwear won't really fit underneath them. But I won't do it if I think there's a chance I'm going to get laid that night. I try to be as clean as I can, and by the end of the day, free-balling balls are not fresh balls. In my experience, most guys who don't wear underwear and have their ass cracks hanging out are dirty dudes.

If you ask me, it's a fairly girly thing for a man to expose his ass crack. You're basically talking about man cleavage. If you're a pretty boy, and you're fit, go for it if you want to. If you're a hairless little pretty boy, some chicks will totally dig seeing your asshole hanging out. But if you have a hairy ass crack, then you need to keep that thing covered.

In general, guys really need to be on top of grooming their body hair. If you've got a unibrow, or some random hairs growing on the back of your arm, then you need to handle that. There's no need for waxing and sculpting, but if you've got hairs where you're not supposed to, or if you've got bum fluff growing on the back of your neck, you've got to tend to that shit.

If you want to have a beard, you need to trim it. If you have a neck beard that just keeps moving south, down into your chest, you just look dirty. Everyone can tell you're not running a tight ship.

It's up to you how much you want to get into removing the rest of your body hair. I don't think you should be too hairy in your private area, especially if you want anyone to put their mouth in that vicinity. If you want girls to start playing with your ass and maybe putting their heads between your legs, I don't think being real hairy and gross is a good idea.

I have been known to keep my body completely hairless. That started out because of skateboarding. I used to have to tape my ankles, and then that would rip all my ankle hair out, so I started shaving around that area. One day I got tired of having a hairline around my ankles, so I shaved up to my knees. But then the new hairline started pissing me off, too. Eventually I just sat there in a backyard in San Diego with a bucket of warm water, and within a couple of hours I had OCD'd myself all the way up to my dick. That was the beginning of me and shaved legs.

Shaving my pubes came a little later. I wasn't getting laid a lot at the time, and I think I wanted to get myself ready for action. Kind of like an "if you build it they will come" type of thing. At first I got my pubes into a kind of triangle shape, but then I decided it looked like I had a vagina. So then I just shaved them off completely. Nowadays I've got a little bit of hair there. But nonetheless, if you blow me you won't get hair in your mouth. And that's really the point of this story.

Shaving my ass hair was the final frontier. That came along when pen shavers were invented. I was always scared to go all the way down there with a shaver, because I didn't want to cut a hole in my ass. And I didn't want to put the clippers in my butt, because you can cut yourself with those, too. But I could always feel a little bit of hair in there, and by this point in time I didn't want any hair anywhere. Over the years, hair has become like dirt to me. It's that OCD thing again. Believe me, it's not like I get any enjoyment from the act of shaving my butthole.

Also, I don't know about you, but I want girls to lick my ass. And

I'm not going to bend over if there's any hair in there. If I was going to lick a girl and she had hair in her ass, then I would probably quit. So why not return the favor? It just seems like common courtesy.

If you want to try shaving your ass, I would advise you to work your way into it. Maybe just trim it the first time with an electric razor. The first couple times I did it, I put my ass up against a mirror. And then I was upside down and on my back, hitting all kinds of positions, trying to figure it out. If you can avoid it, I don't recommend anyone ever look into their own asshole. That got weird for me pretty quick. I don't think my asshole is my best angle.

After watching girls shave their butts, I started to figure out the technique. You don't need a mirror. You feel it out with your hands. It's just like how you would shave the back of your head. I feel for wherever the hair is, and then I run the shaver there. Just keep your fingers near the extra-sensitive bit, and make sure you don't go against the grain. (Yes, the hair on your asshole has a grain.) When you get to the actual hole, I would recommend just hitting it with a pen shaver, because you can easily nick stuff, and as you might imagine, that's not cool. It's very easy to cut your ass, unless you're a pro's pro.

So there you go. My ass is ready for action. My balls are youthful and hairless. And I have a vigorous sex life. Do what you want, but it works for me, and I believe it can work for you, too.

If you don't know what to do with the hair on top of your head, I would recommend just shaving it. No hair is way better than bad hair. If you look like a tosser with a shaved head, then I would go in the other direction and grow it out. If you don't have an advanced-level sense of fashion, then don't go making a statement with your head. If you get a terrible Mohawk, the only people who will talk to you are your bro-dude friends in the terrible-Mohawk club. Whatever style you settle on, you also need to make sure you don't use too much gel. People shouldn't be able to see your skull through your haircut.

If you think you might be going bald, there's a chance it's all in your head. But there's a way better chance that it isn't. Get a really bright light, shine it on the part where it feels like it's thinning, and then shine the light somewhere else on your head. If it's thicker in some places than others, well, then you've got yourself a problem.

I'm told that Rogaine works if you've got the doughnut hole on the back of your head but not if you have a widow's peak. They also say Propecia works if you start it as soon as you know you're going bald. But one of the side effects of Propecia is depression, and then allegedly even if you stop taking it, the depression still might not go away. So I would skip the drugs. And I definitely don't think that anybody should get hair plugs. Nobody has sex with anybody with hair plugs unless the guy is rich. When a rich guy with plugs has a hot girlfriend, she's not fucking his hair plugs—she's fucking his money.

Unless your head is really deformed, if you're going bald, shaving your head is the only answer. It really isn't that big of a deal anymore. Once you know you're thinning, Bic that shit as soon as possible. Girls might fuck dudes who have shaved heads, but they don't fuck dudes who are balding.

I know some guys out there are still rocking bandannas. To each his own, I say. Just know that when you fold that bandanna over your forehead and then spike your hair so it comes out the top, you are advertising to the entire world that you are a raging kook.

The bandanna-kook look is especially offensive if you have bleached hair. I can kind of see bleaching your hair if you're thinning on top and you want to blend your remaining hair in with your scalp. You can go ahead and run that look for a while, until you're ready to face reality and Bic your head. Otherwise, no one should have bleached hair unless they are a woman or a member of Poison.

If you're getting older and you think you can fool everybody by dyeing your hair jet-black, then you are sadly mistaken. First of all, everyone can tell. And secondly, going gray looks awesome and manly, so why bother? If you're a famous movie star and you think you can keep starring in movies for ten more years as long as you dye your hair and get Botox, then go right ahead. But if you're not a movie star and you think you need a dye job and Botox, that tells me and everyone else that you are ruled by your insecurities.

It's very important to always smell good. I shower every day, and twice a day if I go to the gym. I know not everybody is quite that anal. But I also know that if you haven't showered because you're hungover, or because you just came from the gym, or just because you're a scumbag, then you have no right to hit on chicks. In the eyes of society, you are a dirty, sketchy dude, and you're out of the game until you get cleaned up. That may be okay every once in a while. But you never know when life will hand you opportunities. If you take yourself out of the game all the time, you're just making it that much harder to win.

If you're going to wear cologne, the biggest thing is to make sure you're not overdoing it. You don't want the room to smell like you after you leave. If you're not sure how much is too much, find a friend you trust. Have him stand in a room, and then walk in and walk out. If your buddy can still smell you after you leave, then you need to take it down a few notches.

If you can, try to watch a girl put perfume on. Only recently have guys started trying to smell like pussies, but women have been doing it for forever. They're the experts. Plus, men always have to overdo everything. The first times a guy gets his hands on cologne, he's usually going to go off. But that's not how women do it. They just dab a little on their neck and their wrists, and then they're out.

Speaking of women, I have been known to dabble in wearing perfume from time to time. I figure, if girls like the way it smells, then how is it bad if that's how I smell? I used to wear some of my chick's perfume, and girls would always say nice stuff to me. But nowadays, I just smell like my bestie, Benji Madden. Girls stop me and tell me I smell awesome, all the time. It's called Kiehl's Original Musk. You're welcome.

We should probably cover tattoos next, before you do something you're going to regret. The opinions I'm about to share will probably piss off some people who don't want to admit they have bad tattoos. Sorry if the truth hurts, but I need to save people before they unleash yet more insanity on the world. Besides, don't feel bad—I'm the guy who has a tattoo of a shrimp on top of a Barbie doll. Shrimp on the Barbie. Get it? (Although you have to admit, that is kind of awesome.)

If you're going to get a tattoo, don't just randomly get one in Vegas with your buddies. That's a surefire way to end up looking like a fucktard. The most important thing is finding the right artist. Ideally, you should be friends with the artist before you get any work done. That's the safest way to go. If not, when you're ready to jump into the tattoo game, ask people you know who have tattoos. Try to get a recommendation from them. Do some research. Read some magazines. If you don't have any connections, then go to someone with a really good reputation. Yes, it will cost more, and yes, the biggest tattoo artist in your area is probably an asshole. But in the long run it's worth it. You're going to have that thing for a long time.

Once you get to the shop, don't just pick a design off the wall.

Also, if you think you have a really good idea for a tattoo and the tattoo guy says it's a bad idea, you should listen to him. Consider yourself lucky—lots of dudes will just go ahead and put stupid shit on you, because you're paying them.

There are many kinds of horrible tattoos I would personally recommend that you avoid. You probably shouldn't get tattoos of panthers and other wild jungle predators (even though I'm covered with that shit). And tribal tattoos might be the all-time worst. Many people decided that was a great idea in the early nineties, not realizing they were making the biggest mistake of their lives. Tribal is permanently off the list. Unless you are a native of Samoa, in which case, have at it.

If you don't know that you shouldn't get Asian characters, then I probably can't help you. For one thing, you probably don't speak Chinese or Japanese or whatever, so now you're relying on a magazine or a book to get it right. Or, even worse, a tattoo artist. And more importantly, if the word or the phrase that you want is too cheesy to write in English, then Asian characters won't save it. You want a tattoo that says "Strength"? Then get a tattoo that says "Strength." It doesn't make you a deeper individual because you got it written in Morse code.

Whatever you decide to get, I would definitely work my way into tattoos. Nowadays, a lot of people immediately want something everyone can see, so they start somewhere crazy, like their hand. Some people jump right in with full sleeves. That's so dangerous. It's such a huge tattoo, and you've got it forever. I guarantee your first tattoo is not going to be your best one. You're going to have to pay your dues first, like everyone else.

I recently got my head tattooed, which is something I'd been wanting to do for a long time. You definitely don't want to jump into one of those. You need to be sure. It's the same as any tattoo that people can see, really—it's like you're picking out a T-shirt to wear, only you're committing to wearing that T-shirt every day for the rest of your life.

Before you even start, you should plan out your body. If you just get one here and there, when you're shitfaced drunk or when you're at your buddy's bachelor party, then you're just gonna wind up with a bunch of shitty little tattoos. You should really think about it. Each of your tattoos should mean something to you. And you should treat your body like a canvas.

Last but not least, do not get lower-back tattoos. The only time a man should get a lower-back tattoo is when he already has the rest of his back tattooed and he's just getting something to finish it. If you're the funny guy at the party with a tramp stamp, your friends might think you're hilarious. But I guarantee you no one is fucking you.

The way you look isn't the only thing people use to size you up. It's not enough to have decent clothes and an adult haircut and maybe a couple of tattoos. You need to cultivate a general vibe. For example, the music you listen to also says a lot about you. If you drive around with some ludicrous beats coming out of your car, people will hold that against you. The music you listen to also affects the way you see yourself.

Take pop music. It may seem harmless, but I believe it secretly turns a lot of listeners into very angry people. Pop music tells everyone who listens to it that it's cool to own a bunch of shiny things, and spend money, and get laid. But none of the people who listen to that music have any of that stuff. They're never going to drive the car from that video. They're never going to fuck that chick. Hip-hop has gone completely batshit crazy. I don't see how anyone can listen to another song about partying in the club when there is no chance that anyone could ever get into that club in real life. At a certain point, that kind of music has to make you look at your own life and make you pissed.

Guys who listen to techno are also a little suspicious to me. Techno is made for people to listen to when they're on drugs. So I get why people like to listen to it when they party. But when you listen to it outside of the club, I assume that means you want to live in a world where you're constantly on drugs, or that you've done so many drugs that you pretty much *are* constantly high.

I'm not saying you need to listen to the same music as me. But personally, I believe that heavy metal has helped to make me the man I am today. Metal is more pure than other kinds of music. I'm sure behind the scenes it's contaminated by money and the media, just like everything else. But you know the musicians are in it for the right reasons, because there are almost no chicks at their concerts.

And metal is something that real people can relate to. Not because of the lyrics. I have never personally connected with songs about vampires and people biting people's faces off. But it takes a lot of skill and practice for guys to get good at metal. When I was a kid, I remember hearing that Dave Mustaine from Metallica and Megadeth used to sit in his room and play guitar for seven hours a day, every day, for ten years. I could relate to that passion. Hearing that made me want to be that obsessed with skateboarding. It made me want to get so good at something that I didn't have to answer to anyone, just like Metallica.

In particular, I believe that there are only three bands a man ever really needs to listen to: Metallica, AC/DC, and Pantera. For me, Metallica represents manliness, speed, and power. When I first heard them, in Australia, to me they sounded like the American dream. Listening to them made me envision being in America, drinking

Budweiser, and getting paid to ride a skateboard. They showed me the promised land and inspired me to work my ass off to get there. With all due respect, I don't think anyone is ever going to say that about Justin Bieber.

AC/DC is awesome to me for almost the exact opposite reason. Americans might not even be able to appreciate what AC/DC means to someone from Australia. AC/DC means that I'm a tough mother-fucker and I come from a tough neighborhood and I'm proud of it. But no matter where you're from, AC/DC is man music, and nowadays, the world needs as much of that as it can get.

Pantera is a little bit different, because they came along later. They represented all the same things that Metallica did, but they were the evolution of what Metallica had begun. Pantera told me that I also needed to evolve with the times, while at the same time sticking to my guns. Metallica was the theme music of my life, until Pantera's *Vulgar Display of Power*. That album basically refilled the tank of motivation for me. I felt like Phil Anselmo, the singer, knew how to play the game and be the best, and I felt like I could learn from what he had to say. Which, once again, is something very few people are ever going to say about the Black Eyed Peas or Skrillex.

Beyond the way you look and the music you listen to, there are a couple of other things that will instantly inform the world you are a hopeless loser. As I already said in the last chapter, in my mind, one of those things is smoking cigarettes. Do not—I repeat, *do not*—smoke cigarettes. I can't believe people still even need to be told this anymore, but cigarettes cost a lot of money, they make you stink, and they will kill you. (Not *might* kill you. *Will* kill you, if you keep it up.) I could maybe understand it if cigarettes got you high or made your dick bigger, but they don't even do anything. No woman wants to go out with a guy who smokes, unless she smokes. And if the girl you're going out with also smokes cigarettes, that means that she's a moron, too.

Your choice of dog also tells the world a lot about you. Dogs are like hats. Some people can pull off certain hats, and some people can't. To me, most guys who have pit bulls come across as insecure. Guys with pit bulls almost always have cut-off sleeves and a bunch of scary tattoos. That total package usually tells me that they're trying a little too hard to show the world what a badass they are. You know, like me.

And there is not a straight man alive who can pull off a Chihuahua. You need to have conversations with your dog, and a Chihuahua is too nervous to handle a man conversation. If you're a real man and you try to tell a Chihuahua about your day, you will blow his little Chihuahua mind.

If you want a dog that girls will like, you should go with something little. Girls love pugs because they've got mushy faces and a lot of character. The only problem is that pugs can't fight. Any other dog can attack a pug, and the pug will lose. That's why I got a Boston terrier. It's like a 'roided-out pug. It's just a pug with a fighting chance. Or at least a pug with a chance to run away.

The way you spend your free time also tells the world a lot about you. If you want people to take you seriously, you've got to be careful what recreational activities you participate in. I think being seen Rollerblading is a mistake. Hacky Sack isn't going to help you, either. You might find a female Hacky Sack enthusiast or a fellow Rollerblader, and then you two can fall in love, but who the fuck wants to fall in love with a Hacky Sack chick? The same goes for comic books. If I was a guy who liked reading comic books, I wouldn't advertise that fact to about 99 percent of the girls out there. I would keep my comic books hidden in the back of my closet, like they were a stack of German shit-porn magazines.

I also think you should be careful about what kinds of organizations you're affiliated with. Whether you're a Trekkie or part of a fantasy football league of losers, to me it just sounds like a bunch of dudes who stand around eating Cheetos. That's not the vibe you're looking for. A man should have a little mystery about him. And the guy who won last year's fantasy football league is not mysterious.

The only man organization that I personally would be associated with would be a fighting gym. But if you get really into going to the gym and you become a gigantic shredded monster, be careful that doesn't make you forget about all the fashion advice we've already gone over. For example, you should avoid wearing tight T-shirts all the time. I mean, I get it. I know why Vin Diesel feels the need to dress like Vin Diesel. You worked hard to get those muscles, and now you want to show them off. But as a result, you end up wearing some very stupid shit. No one but other big muscle guys thinks that your typical big muscle guy dresses cool.

For some reason, this seems to apply to MMA dudes in particular. Guys who do MMA are very, very tough, but generally speaking they have the style of a dead dog's ass. That's what happens when you're really tough. You don't have time to be a fashionista or to give a shit what your pants look like. That's why a lot of those guys are still guilty of walking around with those crosses on their back jean pockets. They haven't gotten the memo yet that it's over. These are guys who think sweatpants are a sweet look. They're one step away from those bodybuilder dudes who wear fanny packs.

It's impossible to become an extremely massive shredded dude and not pay a price when it comes to style. Not only do none of your shirts fit right, you also lose mobility. There has never been a massive muscle dude who was also an excellent dancer. When you're that huge, you can't even walk right. And that means it is physically impossible to have any swagger.

Obviously, I'm a Neanderthal, and I assume that I'm speaking primarily to my own kind in this book. But I do have a little advice for anybody out there who is not a violent simpleton. Personally, if I was a pussy, I would go the arts-and-crafts route. If I was a skinny, nerdy guy who didn't want to get beat up, I would learn to play the shit out of a musical instrument. You should also try to be hip with the streets and know all the cool zany alternative things to do around town. That will get you a long way in life. Again, confidence is the most important thing, and you can still be confident in your pussy-ism.

A big part of getting your shit together is moving out of Mom and Dad's house. Nowadays, I know it can be really hard to find a job, so I'm going to be really, really friendly and say you have to move out by the time you're twenty-eight. But if times weren't tough, my honest answer would be that you should get out on your own by the time you're twenty-one.

If you're like most dudes, you probably have no idea how to decorate a home. So my advice is to not even try. If you pick a pattern for your couch, you're probably going to pick the wrong one. Just go for a solid color. If you try putting stuff on the walls, you're probably just going to hang up a bunch of posters. And no, it's not any better if your sick poster of LeBron James dunking a basketball is in a frame.

You also need to keep your place neat and clean. And not just sometimes—all the time. You need to take out the trash. You need to wash the dishes. You need to do your laundry, and once your clothes are clean, you need to fold them, too. You should always be ready for a member of the opposite sex to walk into your house. It shouldn't look like a frat party just wrapped up before she got there. You can't have video games and empty glasses everywhere. You need to make your bed every day. And above all else, you need to buy stuff to clean your bathroom with, and then you actually need to use it. You need to scrub the shower and clean the toilet. You need to get rid of that shit that grows on the tiles. Don't think no one's gonna notice if you get lazy and skip the crevices and the corners— those are the grossest parts. If you have a crusty man bathroom, and you have a girlfriend, then I don't care what she told you—I guarantee you she hates it.

If you're going to have a roommate, make sure that he's on board with that same plan for cleanliness. Back in my heyday, I was potentially the worst roommate who ever lived. When I was a skateboarder, I always had roommates. I didn't clean anything, and honestly, that was the least of the problems that came with living with me. I stayed up until four A.M. punching holes in the walls and having sex with girls as loudly as possible. I owned mice that I didn't take care of, so they ate each other to survive and yet still managed to multiply until they started pouring out of the tank. I would bring people over to smoke crack with me, some of whom may or may not have been prostitutes. Sometimes I would wake my roommates up in the middle of the night, asking if I could borrow their credit card to pay for the prostitutes because my card had been declined. As anyone who ever lived with me back then will tell you, you need to choose your roommates carefully.

Finally, if you hate gay people or people of other races, you need to cut that shit out immediately. If you're a racist homophobe, it might not be your fault. Your parents might have raised you that way, or your friends might get off on hating other people. But it's never too late to change. If you don't have any gay friends, you should probably get some. If nothing else, it might help you get laid. Lots of gay guys have really hot chick friends, and some hot chick friends will talk to a random dude who's friends with gay guys. It's like you're sneaking behind enemy lines.

More importantly, if you're homophobic or racist, that just tells me—and any other intelligent person—that you're really angry. It's crazy to me that anyone ever thought it was cool to be that way. But by now everyone has to have gotten the memo. I would like to believe no guy who goes around talking shit about gay people or other races is able to meet women, even though I know that's not true. But what's also a fact is that any girl who thinks it's cute to be racist or homophobic has a very low IQ. This is the kind of woman who will stab you during an argument. It's the chick who's going to cut your dick off when you cheat on her. That's the level of psycho that you're dealing with. That's a dangerous bitch.

That's my closing message for this chapter: You need to open your mind, or else some crazy chick is going to chop your dick off.

3

HOW TO PARTY

NOW THAT YOU ARE NO longer offensive to mankind at first sight, you may be ready to get out of the house and mingle a bit. Next chapter we'll talk about what to do when you're trying to impress girls. But the most basic form of partying is the kind that happens when you and your buddies are just getting shitfaced. So for now, let's go over hanging out, getting loose, and straight-up raging.

I'm in my forties. Nowadays, my idea of a party is eating a ton of pizza and ice cream, watching a bunch of movies, and then making myself throw up at the end of the night to get rid of all the crap I just swallowed. Even if I do go out these days, I've become very spoiled. If I don't have some sort of VIP pass to go somewhere, then chances are I'm not going at all. Of course, it didn't used to be like that. When you're a kid, you don't need to be on a stupid list. You barely even need money. And you know what? Back then, I used to have a lot more fun.

When I was a teenager, all we needed was some beer and a room to drink it in. If we had weed, great. If somebody had some mushrooms or cocaine, then that night was instantly legendary. I don't even remember having mixers for our drinks. Or cups, for that matter. We would just chug straight from the bottles. Vodka. Goldschläger. Jägermeister. Bourbon. It made no difference. Southern Comfort was my personal favorite, because it tasted like candy. You would throw the booze back so hard and so fast that some of it would spray back out of your mouth as your body desperately tried to repel the poison. And then you would do it again.

If you're young and dumb, you may think it's fun to drink Jell-O shots and chug beer through your asshole (that's a real thing, by the way) and draw cocks on your buddy's face after he passes out. And you're absolutely right. All that stuff is awesome and hilarious. (Well, except for butt chugging.) I used to have races with other guys to see who could break the most whiskey bottles over his head. I used to get shitfaced and attempt insane BMX jumps in the middle of the night, and then afterward have a limp for a couple of months. And I don't regret it at all. I think going through a phase where you drink too much is part of what makes you a man.

Part of growing up is learning how to party. Unless you're planning to become a priest or something, you're going to have to learn to handle your alcohol (and your drugs, if you like doing drugs).

Your friends and fellow partiers shouldn't need to hold your hand. The best people I ever partied with were natural leaders, and being wasted brought out the best in them. Take my buddy Sluggo, from the Red Dragons. Back in the day, Sluggo was the kind of guy who always knew where the party was, where to find more booze (and drugs), where everybody could crash for the night, and how to get a taxi when the rest of us were too hammered to figure that out for ourselves. That's the guy you should try to be. That's the guy everybody wants to party with.

Back in my heyday, I was a good example of the guy you did *not* want to be. I was not the leader. Not only was I not the guy who knew where to get a taxi, a lot of times I couldn't even remember where I lived. Colin McKay, another one of the Red Dragons, used to put a piece of paper with his address on it in my pocket, in case I got in a car and didn't know where I was going.

Of course, one of the reasons we were able to party like such humongous assholes is because none of us had any responsibilities. Eventually, you do need to scale it back a bit. The best time to be a drunken moron is when you're in your late teens. I know I shouldn't advocate underage drinking, but as I see it, by the time you're actually legal to buy alcohol (at least in America), that's right about the time you need to cut this kind of shit out.

When you're a kid, to some extent you can get away with that. But once you're in your twenties, it is no longer acceptable to be wasted at all times. Eventually I got my shit together, and if you're a full-grown man, then you need to do the same thing. There are some people who just have a problem. If that's you, then that's something that you need to address real fast. If you drink until you don't know what you did last night, and then there are people you need to apologize to when you wake up, you have to stop.

Also, if somebody you hang out with gets drunk all the time and then flies off the handle, then I would recommend you stop partying with that guy. Not only does nobody want to hang out with that guy, no one wants to hang out with his friends, either.

But that doesn't mean I'm opposed to getting drunk. I feel like being drunk has come to be seen as a bad thing, and I don't agree with that. If you're having a boys' night out, I think it's totally acceptable to get wasted. I don't think it's cool if you get shitfaced all the time and can't handle your booze. And if you're trying to meet girls, I don't think it helps to get wrecked. But when you're out with the boys, or when you're at a barbecue or something, by all means get a proper buzz. Take the edge off. Let your hair down and sing songs with your drunken moron friends and then wake up feeling like shit. I don't see a problem with that.

But if you do get too wasted, you need to know that there is a total etiquette to vomiting. If you are passing out at the same time that you vomit, then the only thing I ask is that you not choke to death on your own puke. But if you're still up and moving around, there are rules that need to be observed. If you know you're about to puke, you need to either get to a toilet or get outside. There is no excuse for vomiting on rugs, vomiting inside automobiles, or vomiting on other people.

If there is no possible way to get to an appropriate vomiting location, then you need to take one for your team and throw up in your shirt. There have been times when I knew that if I tried to stand up, not only was I going to vomit on the floor, I was also going to face-plant or head-butt a wall. But when that's the case, you need to keep your bearings, pull out the bottom of your shirt, and make a little vomit pouch. Sure, your shirt will be done for. But if you're so wasted that you can't get to a safe place to vomit, you were probably going to barf on yourself anyway.

It's also important to pick the right place to party. If your idea of a good time is hanging out at some dude's house and getting wasted with the same bunch of dudes every weekend, I would definitely encourage you to live a little. If you're going to hit a bar, personally, I would lean toward a place where there are at least *some* females. You probably don't want to hang out in an old-man bar. With all due respect to our veterans, there are only so many stories you can listen to about 'Nam.

But more importantly, if you walk into a bar and everybody there is really big and really wasted, then I would advise you to get out of there. If you're the kind of guy who can blend in, you probably don't have anything to worry about. But if you look like me, it's generally only a matter of time before somebody says something to you, or something to your chick, and that's when partying gets very uncomfortable.

People who start fights when other people are trying to party are insecure cocksuckers. There's just no reason for that. If you have differences with another guy, why not invite him to meet you at a gym in the morning, so you can settle things when you're sober? I know why—because you just want to beat up drunk people.

Every now and then, two of these assholes get lucky and find each other and get to have a cocksucker showdown between the two of them. But nine times out of ten, if you're picking fights at a club, you're punching a dude who doesn't want any part of you in the back of the head. I have crazy issues, and I would still never pick a fight at the club. Even if you slapped my chick or called her a slut, I might pop you, but I'm not going to finish you off. I'm not going to foot-stomp you while you're down. I'm going to call the cops or the bouncers and then get on with my night.

Some people might find it hard to believe, but I actually want no part of bar fights. I'll do just about anything to avoid one, particularly if I'm with a girl at the time. That would be my advice to anyone. If a guy starts insulting you, just agree with him. If he tells me I'm a pussy, I back him 100 percent. If he says he wants to smash my pussy face in, I just say, "Whatever I've done, I apologize. I'm not looking for any trouble here." And then me and my chick get up and leave. What else are you going to do? Break a beer bottle over the dude's head and then stab him with broken glass? Forget about the cops and going to jail—is that something you want to live with? I say just walk off like a bitch. Feeling like a bitch is a stinger, but it goes away. Give it twenty-four hours. Maybe the rest of the weekend. In the long run, that's the smarter move.

Sometimes taking the bitch route may not be an option. If a guy wants to corner you, you might be able to run away, but your chick probably can't. If you have tried your best to back down and handle the situation with words, but that will not work, then I say jump on the guy. If this guy is that much of a raging dick, other people will have noticed. It won't be long until strangers jump in to help. Who knows—you might even get a couple shots in before everyone else breaks things up. And in that case, you're getting mad BJs when you get home. Even if your chick says she isn't into violence. Every girl likes violence when it goes down like that. And in her eyes, you just became The Man. But I still recommend you try to get out of there before any altercation goes down. It's just too risky.

I only won one street fight in my whole life. And I've lost a bunch. I've been punched in the chest by people holding keys. I've gotten head-butted by strangers. And based on what I've learned, you're better off losing. Because if you win the fight, you might be going to jail. If you lose a fight, the pain goes away. So what if you looked like a loser in front of a bunch of drunk dudes?

In a street fight, there are no rules. So if you actually want to win, you have to cheat. If you're not prepared to cheat, then you shouldn't be there. Because there's a really good chance that the other guy is. If I was a normal guy without tons of MMA or boxing experience, and there was no way I could back down from fighting some dude, I would say, "Look, I don't want to fight. I don't want anything to do with this. Please don't hurt me." And then I would kick the guy in the nuts and get the hell out of there. Nobody does that. Every single fucking asshole who gets angry in a bar has the exact same game plan: to punch you in the face. No one sees the nut shot coming.

But one more time, let me repeat: It's not worth it. Run away.

Obviously, partying is about more than just drinking and avoiding massive dudes who want to beat you up in front of your chick. While we're on the subject of getting wasted and doing dumb, irresponsible stuff, we should also talk about drugs.

My crazy drug days are long behind me, and I have no desire to ever go back there again. But at my pinnacle, my all-time favorite evening was a drug buffet. There would be weed, boner pills, cocaine, ecstasy, GHB. You name it. I would have tons of red wine to take the edge off the extensive list of drugs I just mentioned. (And, if I was lucky, I would have two chicks there, too.) I had a good solid problem with at least a couple illegal narcotics. So even if I'm over that shit now, I'm an excellent guy to educate you on the subject.

Marijuana barely even counts as a drug anymore, but let's start there. There's definitely a time and a place for a doobie. It's great to get high and, say, go out on a Jet Ski. After you get a girlfriend, it can be great to mellow out and have a few tokes together. The major drawback is that weed makes you a fucktard around other people who aren't as stoned as your dumb ass. You could spin into a paranoid shitstorm that isn't even real.

In general, when it comes to marijuana, if you smoke it but you still get your shit done, you're okay. But if you smoke weed and it stops you from doing what you have to do, then that's the wrong way to do it.

I should add that if you're still a single guy, marijuana does not get you laid. It does not make girls horny. I used to make that mistake all the time. I don't know how many times I got a drunk girl back to my hotel room, only to smoke weed with her until she was throwing up in the sink.

Acid and mushrooms also have no place in the dating scene, although there's a time and a place for them, too. If you're going to take hallucinogenics, you definitely want to do it when you're really young. Once you get to a certain age—maybe twenty—your adult brain starts firing off, and you will lose the desire to leave your rational mind too far behind. That's when the panic sets in. So get them out of the way while you're still young and stupid.

I would do mushrooms over acid, because they're natural. Acid can get pretty sketchy. The safest mushrooms are the ones they put in chocolate, because those come in doses. Eat one bar and then see what happens. And if nothing happens, just wait. You've got plenty of time, and if you take too much, there's no taking it back.

I wish we had had those chocolates back in the day. When I was a boy, back in Australia, you just found mushrooms in the bushes, boiled them in a pot, and then you all kept drinking the tea until somebody started crying. Then we'd all beg for it to go away and have a bunch of out-of-body experiences all night, until I'd wake up the next morning in the bushes, freezing cold, with a bunch of dirt and worms in my pocket and no idea how they got there.

One time, while doing mushrooms in Australia, a guy I was hanging out with announced that he was going into his shoe. He said he looked into the shoe, and the shoe was pulling him in. That's what he told me. And then he never really came out. He was always a weird dude after that. He was always brushing his teeth. He had a toothbrush with him at all times.

Ecstasy is awesome, especially if there's a way you can arrange it so your penis will be inside someone's vagina when it kicks in. Ideally, you would want that person to be attractive. Although back when I used to go on skate tours, I used to take a bunch of ecstasy and then fall in love with the scariest women available. I was kind of famous for that.

If you don't want to have sex with toothless sewer creatures when you're on ecstasy, I have the same advice I'd give you for acid and mushrooms—make sure you're in a safe environment with good friends. Also, you might want to have some nice fuzzy blankets around. (If you don't know why, you'll find out when the pills kick in.) Either way, ecstasy will really burn you out, so you don't want to make it too much of a habit. And do your best to find a good source, so you're not taking any dirty shit. Taking sketchy drugs is like getting sketchy tattoos—only it's not your skin you're messing with, it's your brain.

I definitely don't recommend taking ecstasy alone. I can tell you from experience that's the wrong move. Here's a quick story:

One time, back in Melbourne, somebody got me like four pills. They were really good ones. I arranged to go somewhere to get laid, but then I took them on my way over, and they kicked in faster than I expected. It got too hot and heavy for me on the road, so I pulled over.

And then I sat in a rent-a-car for like four fucking hours, smoking back-to-back blunts. I remember I could hear myself breathing, and it sounded like I was coming, although I was way too high to jerk off. I had to sit there until they wore off enough for me to continue on my way, and by then it was too late.

I only took PCP once. I was up in Vancouver living with the Red Dragons, and there were these two chicks who ran the Red Dragons' clubhouse. I took PCP with one of them, and next thing I knew I was duct-taping her to a chair. I remember she was laughing a lot, so I duct-taped her mouth shut, too. (Mind you, this was a consensual duct-taping. She was laughing her ass off the whole time.) At some point, the chair fell over, and she was on her back, and I started squirting mustard and ketchup all over her. By the time anyone else showed up, I was on a couch and she'd been on the floor for like an hour. They were like, "What are you doing?" And I was like, "Squirting this chick with condiments. What does it look like?" Then they untaped her. She wasn't mad. Don't forget, she was on angel dust, too. If that sounds like your idea of a good time, then by all means look into PCP.

If you want to know the right time to do painkillers, the correct answer is when you break a bone. The doctor gives them to you and then you take the amount that it says to on the bottle. And that's it. I know a lot of kids do pills these days, and that's completely terrifying to me. If you are a young person reading this book, I don't know how to say this in a nice way: You are too fucking dumb to take painkillers socially. You will get fucking addicted to them. And then you will ruin your life.

I know some seemingly rational people who like taking a pill every now and then. But if you think you're taking too many pills,

I would tell you the same thing I would tell a person who might be overdoing it with any drug: Don't do it for thirty days. If you can't lay off it for thirty days, then you have a problem.

That brings us to the really legendary bangers of the drug world, starting with cocaine. I'm not going to lie: in my opinion a little cocaine can be fun. Sprinkling a little cocaine on top of a party has been known to liven up the room.

First of all, if I was going to do cocaine for the first time, I would do the littlest bit ever. I would start with an amount that barely even counts. And I wouldn't care what anyone said about that. There's a type of guy out there who does one line of cocaine and then just dies. It's the same as the people who take mushrooms and then never come back. So you need to make 100 percent sure you're not that guy.

One of the nice things about cocaine is that coke whores will always respond to it. And coke whores fuck like animals. Here's a quick coke whore tip: Take the girl to the bathroom, then sprinkle some coke on the top of the toilet. After she snorts that, sprinkle it on your dick, and then put your dick in her hand. I absolutely guarantee you she will go along with it every time. Just make sure she does it quick, because if you leave coke on your dick it burns. (Don't ask me how I know that.)

Cocaine is no big deal if you do a line while you're drinking at a party, and then you celebrate a bit and then go home and go to sleep. But if you arrange to have it before you go out, that's bad. If you get cocaine and then you don't even bother going out anymore, that's really bad.

The problem with cocaine—and really, the problem with any drug—comes when you're no longer just trying to take the edge off or enhance the mood. You're taking the drug for the sake of taking the drug. That will lead you to some places that you probably weren't intending to go.

One time, I was hanging out in Reno with a bunch of dudes who will remain nameless. We were drinking in a Jacuzzi and doing a ton of coke. We had the keg right next to the water so we didn't have to get out. It was freezing outside, and we were all naked, and we started betting each other over who would run farthest out of the Jacuzzi. And yes, that's a little bit gay. It got to the point where one of us was trying to get over the fence and into the neighbor's yard. Naked. In the snow.

We kept knocking glasses over into the water. None of us thought much about that until the water in the Jacuzzi started turning red. It took us a while to realize it was blood. Apparently we had been stepping on the glasses and breaking them. All the broken glass had settled on the bottom, but we were so gakked out, we didn't realize we had been shredding our feet. We were wading in our own blood, for God knows how long. I don't necessarily blame cocaine entirely. We were also really drunk, which might have dulled the pain. And we'd all been up for days. But then again, the only reason we'd been able to stay up for days and keep drinking was because we were doing blow. So ultimately you still have to consider cocaine the main culprit here.

And coke dealers are heavy, man. There are some pussy lightweight coke dealers, but those are just the ones who haven't been arrested yet. When they face some legal consequences once or twice, they know what they're risking, and after that, they are not fucking around. If you have a coke dealer, he might want to bullshit a bit when he sells you stuff, but my advice would be to spend as little time around him as possible. He probably has a gun, and there's a good chance he's drunk or high a lot of the time. You don't want to be friends with your coke dealer. That's a bad friend to have on so many levels, because once you're buddies, you can call him at all times, and he'll actually show up. Which is a perfect way to get a massive cocaine addiction. If you can't maintain a professional relationship with your coke dealer, then you shouldn't be doing cocaine.

Crystal meth is a lot like coke, only way worse. While I do think there's a time and a place for cocaine, it's harder to make that argument for crystal. The only time crystal meth can help you is when you're about to have sex and you want to put on a show. If you've never had sex on crystal before, you might consider taking a Viagra or a Cialis or something like that first. You might be fine without the boner pill, but on the other hand, when the crystal kicks in, you might not be able to get it up. And then you might not get it up until the crystal wears off, which is going to be quite a while.

The worst thing about sex on crystal meth is that it takes so long. I smoked meth out of a lightbulb with a hooker one time and then had sex with her until she basically tapped out. She was like, "I'm sorry. I am done." And I still hadn't ejaculated. I jacked off in a cold shower for an entire day afterward. I had to change masturbation techniques, because my penis had become deformed from overuse. It looked like a mushroom.

Back in my crystal meth prime, I'd go off on a binge for maybe a week at a time. I'd come back maybe fifteen pounds lighter. When I was on crystal meth, if I didn't have someone to have sex with, then I had to jerk off constantly. I could not stop. I'd disappear into the bathroom for like eight hours at a time. I remember jerking off a flaccid pee-pee at times, because I had methed my boner into submission. And I was happy doing it. Joyful. Needless to say, it's a pretty weird time to look back on. (I will say this, though—there is no satisfaction in a job well done like the feeling you get when you finally drop a load after jerking off for an entire day.)

The even bigger pitfall of crystal meth as a lifestyle is that your friends are going to rob you, constantly. It's only a matter of time before everybody that you do crystal meth with will only be thinking about getting crystal meth. They won't even know you anymore. Meth is really cheap, but that only makes it worse, because that means cheap people do it.

In summary, I've had some of the best sex of my life on crystal. I once fucked the same chick around the clock for two days straight. But I can also tell you that sex is awesome on crack. I don't think that means you should do either of them. The comedown from crystal is so brutal. You think the darkest stuff, until crystal has taken away your will to live. It's just about the worst drug ever.

Except, perhaps, for heroin. At one point in my life, I used to get hookers, which I enjoyed immensely. And then I used to get hookers and do heroin with them. Then I stopped doing the hookers and just started getting high on heroin by myself. So I don't really see how that worked out for me. The only thing heroin is really good for is helping you write songs about heroin. Allow me to be the one billionth person to say it: Don't do heroin.

Finally, there is crack: There is no right way to do crack. End of story.

A lot of people who are reading this book are going to try drugs, if they haven't already. I'm sure there are some high people reading this right now. It's totally understandable to experiment. As you can see, I did my fair share.

I don't regret trying any drugs. If they don't get in the way of the other stuff you need to handle, then who cares? But when you start making a drug into a lifestyle, that's when it's a problem. It doesn't matter all that much whether it's alcohol or crystal—you can't make an everyday, constant habit out of any of them.

I remember what it feels like to need cocaine, and I don't remember that feeling being good. I remember being in Australia, already stinging to get back to America, which is where I did cocaine. (Cocaine is shitty in Australia, and it's so expensive there that I couldn't afford it anyway.) When I was going back to America, cocaine was in my head when I got in the taxi to go to the airport. It was on my mind during the first flight and through the connecting flight, then on the train from LAX, straight through to the car ride from the train station to my dealer's house, down by San Diego. Throughout that entire trip, pretty much the only thing I was thinking about was putting blow up my nose.

Being that fucked up is a really lame waste of time, and that's assuming you don't destroy your life in the process. If you're an adult and partying is the main thing you look forward to on a daily basis, you're probably overdoing it. When you're a kid, you can go way over the top with partying and you still might not wake up with a crazy hangover. You might still be able to go to school or do your job. You can pull it off. But in my experience, the farther you go into partying, the harder it can become to get out of it. If you stay in the hard-core partying game too long, eventually somebody's getting pregnant, or somebody's going to jail, or both. You've got to be careful, or else you end up selling drugs, having babies with people who don't like you, and getting assault charges.

If you want to party the right way, in my mind you're better off just sipping a couple of beers and trying to get laid instead. Which leads us into chapter 4.

HOW TO GET LAID

IF YOU'VE MADE IT THIS far, you now know how to get fit and how to party. If you've got some proper clothes and a haircut, and you're able to handle your drugs and alcohol without embarrassing yourself, then congratulations—that means there's a decent chance you are now eligible to get laid. We'll cover relationships and falling in love and all that other bullshit later on. For now, it's just about getting yourself out there and meeting as many women as possible.

If you don't have much experience with sex, you should know

that it comes with a price. Sex usually ends up involving a bunch of drama. And it also comes with a lack of sleep. Chicks generally don't agree to go home with you at six thirty in the evening. I'm pretty sure that if they did a survey for one-night stands, the average start time would be way past midnight.

If you don't want to get laid all the time, then maybe it's not worth the effort for you. Thanks to modern technology, you can spank yourself silly on the Internet. It's there, it's free, and you don't even have to leave the house. But if you make that decision, you're missing out on the thrill of the hunt. You're missing out on all the late nights and sunrises and cool things that only happen when you're still up at five A.M., trying to get laid. Some nights will be better than others, but it's almost always an adventure. There is also a sense of accomplishment that comes with sealing the deal. And that never goes away, no matter how many times you get a woman to agree to have sex with you.

One time, when I was on a skate tour in my early thirties, I managed to have sex with a giant lady. She was not all that hot, but she was way over six feet tall, and to me, that meant I had to have her. I met her in a bar and then managed to take her into an alleyway. It was awesome. Nobody found us there, but the gigantic chick definitely thought it was really hot and kinky that we were doing it out back like that. I had to fuck her on a stairwell, standing a couple steps higher than she was, because she was so much taller than me. And, my friend, if I have to explain to you why that is glorious, then you might be reading the wrong book. That's the kind of adventure that can be waiting for you if you get out of the house and go mix it up.

Nowadays, personally I mainly get laid thanks to Twitter and Instagram. Girls hit me up and say that they think I'm hot, because they've heard me on the radio or seen me on TV. Although despite what you might think, I do not get laid because I drive a Porsche. That has not happened one time ever, at least not yet. Things might be different if I didn't live in Hollywood. But where I live, my car is like a fucking Acura. No one gives a shit.

If you don't have girls hitting you up on Twitter or a radio show where you can meet porn stars, don't take it too hard. You've got to start somewhere. My first piece of advice would be to go online and see who's out there. Especially if you still feel awkward about striking up conversations with complete strangers in public.

Personally, I dropped out of school at a young age. I used to skateboard all day, by myself. Nobody knew me. I didn't talk to anyone. So I remember deciding that I was just going to ask people out. I approached any girl I saw that I had even a remote interest in. Sometimes I would get ten sweet shutdowns in a row. But I didn't care.

You probably don't even need to work as hard as I used to. Thanks to the Internet, it's easier than it's ever been to find chicks. Promiscuous married cougars. Hot and horny grandmothers. IWanttoFallinLove.com. Try them all. Mix it up. Don't worry about getting shut down. That's part of the fun. It's just like when you start working out. You need to embrace your cluelessness.

When you're just getting started, the whole idea is to experience as much as you possibly can. When I was seventeen, I had sex with an old lady at a skateboard event. She was a nice lady, but she was maybe forty-five and she was not hot. But on the other hand, I had no idea what I was doing, and she was a pro's pro. So things kind of evened out. She took me in the bathroom and did all kinds of weird shit. That was the first woman who ever smacked my boner on her face. I walked out of that bathroom a changed man. I believe that sensation is what every man should be looking for.

You need to be honest with yourself about how attractive you are and then adjust your goals accordingly. If necessary, lower your standards. Why not? What makes you so sure that you're so hot anyway? If you don't have a lot of experience, you're only going to get so far. You can live in a fantasy world and tell yourself anybody has a chance with anybody. But that's not the case. If you're not rich or devastatingly handsome (or both), in the beginning you should only shoot so high. Even if you think you're already shooting low, if it's not working out for you, then you need to try shooting even lower than that. There's someone out there for everyone. But sometimes, that someone for you might end up being a little hideous.

If you're at a bar or a club and you want to approach a woman, you need to know how to carry yourself. I shouldn't need to tell anyone these next few things, but just in case: Don't scratch your ass in public. Don't pick your nose. No burping and farting. That's just obvious.

When you're hanging out, you also don't want to get caught staring in the mirror styling your face. Men aren't supposed to be concerned about that. Of course, we are. But you can't be looking in mirrors everywhere you walk or else you look like a kook. If your getup is wobbly, you need to fix your shit before you leave the house.

The number one key to being cool is confidence. If you feel like you don't know how to party, or if you're awkward around a lot of people, you're not alone. God doesn't just hand everybody the natural ability to work a crowd. If you feel shy when you meet new people, don't fake it. It's okay if you don't have a ton of witty things to say. Just don't curl up in a ball and call it a day. Make an effort. Try to at least be a little outgoing.

On the other hand, there are definitely people out there who should talk less. If you think that might apply to you, you're probably right.

Drinking to loosen up a bit is fine. But drinking heavily to get confidence is not a good idea. If you get a little nervous talking to people, that's not necessarily a bad thing. Embrace the nerves. Nerves can sharpen you up. Being a little too anxious might screw you up a bit at first, but if you have to get shitfaced to go talk to somebody, then I promise you that approach isn't going to work out, either.

Some people might tell you that a dude should only drink manly beverages like beer or whiskey. I don't think that's really the case. I order Shirley Temples all the time, and chicks dig it. It's more about how you carry your drink. If you're going to drink a fruity drink in front of a girl, you just need to own it. Give me a motherfucking Shirley Temple, and make it a double.

When you're at the bar, I don't think playing pool all night or being on the dart team is a good idea. Playing pool and playing darts is acting like you're already a washed-up married guy. Right now, you're trying to mix it up and hopefully get laid. It's okay if you want to have a boys' night from time to time, but in general I don't think bar games are a good idea. There will be plenty of time for that later, when you're old and lame.

When it comes to approaching a chick, the first thing you need to do is establish eye contact. If a girl looks back at you, then be ready to go for it immediately. Girls know how it works. They know that every time they make eye contact with a male inside any place that serves alcohol, they're triggering a horny moron to come over to them. So they're not going to waste it. You might catch a girl's eye once by accident, but if it happens twice, it's because she wants to talk to you. So get over there.

I wish I could give you a magic pickup line that works every time, but magic pickup lines don't exist. No ugly dude has ever approached a girl who wasn't interested in him and changed her mind with some cheesy line. Even if by some chance a line works, it's because there was already some physical attraction. You don't need a line. You just need to strike up a conversation as fast as you can, before she gets bored and ditches you.

When it comes to conversation, you have to find a balance between not being a dick and not being too nice. If the chick says something you don't agree with, then don't tell her that you do. If you get caught doing that, you're fucked. So stick to your guns. If I believe in something, I'm not going to lie to get laid. (Until you get back to her place. If you're that close to sealing the deal, feel free to lie your ass off, if necessary.)

If the girl you're talking to wants a drink, you need to buy it for her. I would not take no for an answer. I always pay for drinks, because that's what a gentleman does. If you're having a drink together, then you're off to a good start. You want to be careful not to be sloppy and spill your cocktail on her. And you really need to make sure you don't drink too much. You might be nervous, and she might be nervous, too. But pace yourself. Mix in a water here and there. At this point, the object of the game is not to get hammered. You're trying to have fun, potentially get a phone number, and maybe even get laid. If you strike out and end up alone for the night, there will be plenty of time later to drown your loser sorrows.

If you get a phone number and you want to text a girl, you want to do it in a way that does not embarrass the entire race of men. There is no place for "LOL" in any man's text messages. When a man wants to express amusement in a text message to a woman, he should either say "ha" or "ha ha." Really, that's it. "Ha" actually means that the little joke she just made is boring me. Sometimes a girl needs to know that you're not a super-giddy pushover who's too excited that she's talking to you. "Ha" keeps her in check a little bit.

"Ha ha" means that what she said was actually really funny, and you appreciate it.

Yes, this shit is complicated. Yes, it's ridiculous. And yes, you really do need to know this stuff.

If you want to go to nightclubs instead of bars, the most important thing is finding the right club. If there's no line at the club, then that club probably sucks. Nobody likes standing in line, but if there are a ton of people waiting to get inside the place, and some of them are hot women, then that's the place you want to be.

If you wait in line and then the bouncer doesn't let you in, don't get mad. That guy did you a favor, because if you don't look cool enough to get in, then none of the women inside were going to talk to you anyway. You were going to waste your money on overpriced drinks for nothing.

If you do make your way past a bouncer and get inside a club, you might think you're supposed to dance, since there's incredibly loud music playing and a bunch of other people are doing it. But you would be wrong. If you don't know how to dance—and that applies to most straight men—then don't do it. If you're talking to a girl, there's a good chance she will want you to dance. You can't be a dick about it, obviously, but you've got to stand your ground. No means no. I mean, you could slow-dance. Because then all you have to do is just grab her hips and hold on. But otherwise, many a potential one-night stand has died a sad quick death out there on the dance floor.

Even if you are a great dancer, I would keep that to myself. I don't think you score a lot of points by showing off your sick moves. Being a really great dancer actually kind of makes it worse. I have witnessed men execute spin moves and full-on backflips on the dance floor and then go home with no one. Meanwhile, I was watching them from the bar, where I was talking to chicks who went home and had sex with me.

The bar is your friend. That's where you go. That's where you stay.

I would recommend you not be the guy who takes his shirt off at the club. First of all, people are really anal these days. If you get wasted and whip your shirt off, you're going to be escorted off the premises. And rightly so. If you pull that move on the dance floor, you're telling me that either you're not getting laid tonight or you have a girlfriend who's currently embarrassed to be seen with you.

If I wanted to get laid tonight, and I couldn't just ring up somebody in my phone, personally I would head out to the trashiest pub I could find. Girls at nightclubs are hard work. But girls at pubs aren't all dressed up, and they don't take themselves so ridiculously seriously. And most of the time girls at pubs really enjoy their cocktails, which means their vibe tends to be on the loose side.

After I got a drink, I would look around everywhere to see if there was anyone who was slightly interested. I would wait for someone to do the double-look thing, and once that happened, I'd go right up to her and buy her a drink.

Naturally, it would be nice if the girl was really pretty. All guys like pretty girls. But that's not the main thing I'm looking for. Pretty, boring girls are great, if that's what you're into, but picking up chicks can be hard work, and in my experience, pretty girls aren't worth it. I don't care if somebody sees me with a hot chick and thinks that makes me cool. I've put the work in with super-pretty girls, and it's not that good. I've been there. I'm over it. I am looking for an animal. The perfect girl for me to meet at a bar would be someone who punches me in the head and then pulls my pants off when I fall over.

I'm actually almost in fear of chicks that the normal world considers super hot. I feel like most of those girls are up their own asses a lot of the time, and if I dated them, they would spend all of their time complaining about their lives and posting photos of themselves on Instagram. I have a major thing against people who think they're above everyone else. I would break up with the hottest chick on the planet if I found out she was like that.

In terms of looks, I would much prefer a girl who looks evil over someone who looks like a chick from a sitcom. I'm attracted to girls who are covered in tattoos. I like girls who are like me. A lot of times, I don't even decide if a girl is attractive. My penis does it for me. My penis has a way of sniffing out horny sex maniacs. Those are the girls who would inspire me to put in the effort.

Once I approached a girl at a bar, then I'd start telling jokes. Trying to be really romantic or sexy right off the bat comes across really creepy.

Once you do that, there's an easy way to tell if a girl likes you. If she starts telling you all about herself or bragging about anything, she's doing it because she finds you interesting and wants you to be interested in her, too.

There are two warning signs I would look for if I was talking to a chick I just met in a bar. If a girl doesn't make a lot of eye contact, that tells me that she doesn't give a shit. But on the other hand, it's always a little scary to me when a girl always has her eyes wide open. It's like she's trying to see inside your soul. That tends to weird me out, even though sometimes girls with crazy eyes are good in bed. In summary, you're looking for a girl who makes eye contact, but not a girl who gives you a creepy staredown.

If I feel like I have the green light from a girl I'm talking to, I'll move in for a kiss really fast. We're already talking, and now we're sitting together at the bar. So why wait? If a girl is willing to make out with me, I don't wait more than twenty minutes. I've always been like that. It's amazing my face isn't covered with herpes.

Drinking establishments and the Internet are the obvious places to try to meet women, but there are plenty of other options. Going to a restaurant by yourself is a pretty cool way to pick up chicks, because you look so lonely. Waitresses love that. And supermarkets work for me all the time. I mean, I don't go to supermarkets specifically to hit on chicks, but if I'm already there doing some shopping and I see someone I like, then I go for it. As long as you're not a dick about it, women find it very flattering if you approach them in a store. It's really quiet, so it's potentially very embarrassing for you if you get shut down. It's that confidence thing again. Chicks like it because they know you're going for it. And they don't see it coming.

Confidence really is everything. After I got divorced, a couple of years ago, I was so down on myself that I couldn't get laid. I thought I sucked, and so that's how I carried myself. The turning point came when I started dating my girlfriend. She told me I could sleep with other people if I wanted to. But I still had her to go home to, so now I had nothing to lose. I could say whatever I felt like saying to whoever I wanted, and I could be completely honest. If I did that and a girl still wanted to fuck me, then that was awesome. But if she didn't, I didn't give a shit. And it worked. I was the same guy the whole time, but the way I carried myself changed the outcome completely.

You should definitely get in the habit of checking for wedding or engagement rings before you hit on a chick. Although, even if you forget, as long as her husband isn't standing right next to her, she'll probably just say thank you and then inform you that you're an idiot. But even in that case, it was still good practice for you, and you still probably made her day. You can't lose.

There are plenty of guys who figure out a way to talk to girls and to get girls to like them. But then they only end up being friends with everybody. If you meet a girl at a bar and end up in the Friend Zone, that means you came at her the wrong way. Guys get put in the Friend Zone because they are pussies.

Some girls love having guy friends they don't have to fuck. That's why girls love gay guys. I've never really understood why. Maybe it's one of those things you can only understand if you have a vagina. I guess they like to talk about their problems and get some feedback from a male perspective. For a lot of girls, it's also an ego stroke to know that a man wants to bang her, but she gets to just keep him around as a friend. Some girls love that. Again, I don't know why.

Most of the time, I don't think men and women really can be friends. I mean, I can be friendly with my friend's wife. If I see some of my friends' wives at a bar, I can sit down and bullshit with them for an hour, no problem. But I don't go out to lunch with my friend's wife. I don't text to her to see how her day's going.

Generally, when a single guy and a single girl are friends, there's sexual tension coming from at least one side of the friendship. Maybe not always. If your best friend is a big fat lady who is forty years older than you and smokes a pipe, I can see how that could work. But if you want to bone your chick friend, or your chick friend wants to bone you, then you need to discuss that. Otherwise, that tension will just be there forever. And I don't understand why people would want to live like that.

If you do find yourself in the Friend Zone, I say you should just make out with your friend and see what happens. Because if you really like that girl, you're wasting time, and you're torturing yourself, and you're not getting anything out of it. If you kiss her and things get awkward and then you guys aren't friends anymore, that's probably for the best. You needed some kind of forward movement. You needed to force the issue and make something happen.

The exact opposite of the Friend Zone is the rare but awesome occasion where you get to fuck a stranger. Sometimes, when you're out trying to meet girls, if you're lucky, you might be able to skip the small talk and get right down to business. The most basic way sex can come together is when you just look at someone and you know it's on. I'm not gonna lie—this doesn't happen everywhere I go. But any time it's ever happened, I just knew it. There's an instant connection. She looks at me, and I look at her, and I get this feeling that we'd be really good in bed together. And I'm pretty sure she's thinking the same thing.

It can happen anywhere, but let's say you're at a party. If I feel like we're giving each other that look, then why try to hide it? I don't say anything. I'll just kiss them. Of course, if you're wrong here, there's a good chance you'll have to go find somewhere else to party. But any time I ever got that vibe, I never had to apologize.

If you're going to agree to have sex over the course of a two-minute conversation, it doesn't matter where you take her—the bushes, an alleyway, maybe the bathroom. There's a serious connection there, and it's going to be one fiery jam session, for however long it lasts. It's probably going to be crazy. You're going to be living the dream—flicking panties off to the side and saying a bunch of weird shit back and forth with this complete stranger you're now having sex with.

If this should ever happen to you—and I hope that it does—know that by no means does this mean you're suddenly boyfriend and girlfriend for the night. In my experience, you usually end up walking away from each other immediately afterward. Usually, she goes back to her friends at the party and I go back to mine. Unless the sex is really good. In that case, we probably don't go back to the party at all. You don't say good-bye to your friends. You just head to the car or your house or wherever you're planning to continue boning.

Unless your name is Prince, there's no way you can force the spontaneous sex connection to happen. In my whole life, it's come together maybe five times. Most of the time, what you're trying to achieve is your more traditional one-night stand.

As I've said, I'm not much of a bar guy these days. So to have a one-night stand, generally I would start by inviting a girl to dinner. The number of women in the world that I want to fuck is way higher than the number of women I really want to have dinner with. So, ladies, if I'm having dinner with you, you can safely assume that I'm down to take things farther.

If a girl is willing to have sex on the first night, then sign me up. But I don't expect it, and I make sure she knows that I don't expect it. If at some point during dinner she indicates that she's decided to go for it, then I act very surprised and very flattered. Otherwise, after dinner, all I want to do is make out with her.

Because that's where I'll get her.

If a guy makes out with a girl, that means he wants to have sex with her. But if a girl makes out with a guy, that might be as far as she's planning to go. A lot of them will even say it. "Look, I can tell you right now you're not getting any." That's fine by me. I'll tell her I don't want to sleep with her, either. Which is bullshit. But sometimes it's part of the dance.

Not that long ago, I went to somebody's house to take her to dinner. I was sitting in her living room. She bent over to fix something, and her dress rode up. It was obvious she was trying to show me her panties. So I said, "Are you serious?" She played dumb. And this girl was a Penthouse Pet. I was like, "Do you want me to just jump your bones right now, or do you want to wait until after dinner?"

And she said, "I can tell you right now that you're not getting any tonight."

I told her that was okay with me. And then we made out. Then she was like, "We should really go to dinner."

Again, I told her that was okay, but I also told her to kiss me one more time before we left. And then I put my hand on her neck, and did a little rubbing and then a little groping, and then, before you knew it, she wanted us to electrocute each other a little bit. She had this toy you can use to zap people. It's actually kind of cool.

Now, mind you, she told me she just wanted to play a little game. I was told explicitly that sex was still not on the table. But every time it was my turn to zap her, I played it hard. I put her as close to the orgasm zone as possible. She was definitely warming up to the idea of boning. But I still didn't do anything dumb. I didn't say, "Let me just put in the tip." Do not ever fucking say that. I just kept winding her up.

That's what you do. Just rile her up. Get her pants wet, and then let her make her decision. I just get them to the point where they've come in their panties a couple times, and I'm like, "Well, see you later. You said you didn't want to have sex tonight. I'm just trying to be respectful."

She will probably call you on your bullshit. And so you have to commit to that angle. "I am perfectly okay with not having sex with you. Watch me walk out the door right now."

By this point, we were naked, but I was genuinely okay with not fucking her. I think chicks dig it when a man has the self-control to do that. If you're a young, inexperienced dude, you're probably not capable of getting naked in bed with a Penthouse Pet and then just saying, "Oh well," and putting your pants back on. I was okay with not putting my penis inside her, and that's why she wanted me to do it.

I never made it to dinner with that chick. She ended up being really into me for a long time. She knew I had a girlfriend the whole time, but I still had to get a big tattoo of somebody else's name on my wrist to get her to call it a day.

And now she hates me. Unfortunately, that is also a part of getting out there and getting laid. Sometimes, in the long run, it makes girls hate you.

5

HOW TO HAVE SEX

IF YOU'VE MADE IT UP to chapter 5, perhaps that means a woman has agreed to have sex with you. Congratulations—you've come a long way, champ.

For starters, let me say that being awesome at sex isn't a skill you either have or don't have. And getting laid all the time doesn't necessarily mean that you have the ultimate sex life. Like almost everything else in life, sex is something you can make yourself better at, as long as you set your mind to it. In my opinion, most people aren't getting nearly as much as they can out of their sex lives. And that includes a lot of people who are having sex all the time. I'm not talking about the amount of sex people have—I mean the quality.

I believe that the reason most people don't have amazing sex is because most people don't really care about it all that much. They've decided they're okay with pumping away under the covers in the dark for ten minutes at a time. That must be the case—because otherwise, they would do something about it.

I'm obviously at the extreme end when it comes to sex drive. But I think everyone has an instinct somewhere inside them to tap into the beast and fuck like an animal. I think some people are shy, and that keeps them from doing the kinds of things they really want to do or asking their chick to try something new. It's a hard subject to even discuss with a lot of people, because they'll lie to you. They'll tell you that they're content having mediocre sex. You have to break through so many walls and barriers to get them to admit that there are some issues in their sex life. It's like trying to get a junkie to admit they have a problem with drugs.

I think people worry too much about the way they look. That's a big one. People don't want to show other people that when they bend a certain way, they're giving you a bad angle to look at. But most people have bad angles. Even hot chicks have bad angles. I feel like letting that go is one of the keys to having good sex.

When I've been with people who aren't good in bed, the main thing I've noticed is how insecure they are. They're worrying about whether their stomach is too fat. Or a girl has a couple crooked teeth, so whenever she's close to coming, she needs to cover her mouth. Guess what—I already noticed your teeth. And I don't care. That's why I'm having sex with you and trying to get you off. Forget about your teeth and let yourself go.

If you're a dude and you're not that attractive, fuck it. Unless you're so out of shape that it literally affects your stamina, who cares? I've had sex when I was in shape and when I was out of shape, and I don't think it really affected the way the girl looked at me. Put your humongous belly on top of her and just go for it.

I'm in my forties, and I would say that I am currently having the best sex of my life. Looking back to when I was a kid, I had no idea what I was doing. But over the years, I have had a lot of practice. Here is what I've learned:

The best kind of sex starts way before you and your chick are even in the same room. I am a big fan of text sex. That's a great way to start building the mood while you're going through your day and handling other shit. Text sex is particularly good if people are a little bit shy. Lots of girls find it hard to say slutty things in person. But for some reason it's easier for them to talk about gagging on your cock if they're typing it on their phone.

When a girl goes above and beyond like that, that's really fucking hot to me. The more details she includes, the more I know she's really thought about it. Sexy texts are a gift that keeps on giving. I get to look at that text over and over, whenever I have a spare minute, until I get home. If you're at work and your boss is yelling at you, it's very empowering to know that you have a text in your phone about how some chick can't wait to try to swallow your genitals.

Once you get into the bedroom, it's important to set the right mood. Personally, I don't understand why anybody wants to have sex with the lights off. First of all, if you don't know your partner very well and they want the lights off, to me there's a chance they have something scary and contagious on their privates that they don't want you to see. But more importantly, why would you not want to see the person you're fucking? You should be trying to stimulate all of your senses, and if you're fucking in the dark, you're shutting down a pretty big one.

However, I don't think it's a good idea to have the lights on really bright. Strip clubs are dark for a reason. I don't think bright lights are really flattering to anyone, including myself. Everyone's a little deformed. Girls have random hairs on the nipples and stuff like that—even the hot ones. So go for mood lighting.

Assuming we are now moving into the bed area, here is a quick reminder for guys: If you pull your pants off, your shoes and socks have to come off, too. Wearing socks in bed is an amazing move, and yet sometimes I still see guys with their socks on in porn. I'm like, "Dude, you know they're filming this, right?" There's literally not one man alive who could look sexy with just his socks on. Matthew McConaughey naked with socks on is not an attractive man.

Once you've started making out, the next logical move is to grab a titty. When you grab a titty, I say you've got to grab it like a man. Don't just brush your hand over it. Don't act like you didn't do it. You've got to go for it with gusto.

But that doesn't mean you need to apply a death grip. Some chicks like it when you pinch their nipples or twist them, but I wouldn't get too happy on those moves, at least off the bat. Even if someone's being really aggressive toward me, I'm trying to avoid scaring her until I've got a full read on the situation. (Although once I'm sure she's into extreme nipple play, I ain't scared to slap a titty.)

Hopefully no one who's reading this book is still using the old-school finger-blast maneuver during foreplay. Occasionally, you might want to break out the finger blast if you've already been having sex for a few hours. And it definitely comes in handy if you're fucking two or three chicks at the same time. But otherwise, a

This is me looking extremely awesome.

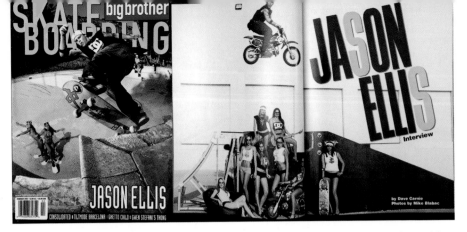

A magazine shoot from about ten years ago. I thought it would be funny if I could make it look like two chicks were underwater while I skated this pool. (I know what you're wondering right now: I only boned one of them.)

Mike Blabac

I got to test drive all the 2013 450s, thanks to *Motorcycle USA* magazine. Sometimes I feel very lucky that I get to be me.

Justin Dawes Photo

My first time behind the wheel of a Super Lite truck. The announcer called me Yardsale, because I rolled so many times I left parts of my truck all over the track.

Ryan Steely / www.ryansteely.com

Eighteen-foot Method Air, back in the day. You might not know what that means, but trust me— it's awesome.

Jody Morris Photo

At an Ellismania weekend in Las Vegas, performing with my band
Death! Death! Die! I am possibly the worst lead singer on earth
who gets to perform live in front of thousands of screaming fans.

Jayson Steele Fox

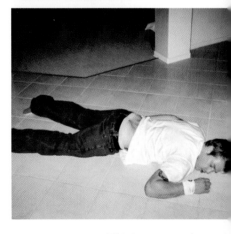

How not to party. This is me passed
out on the floor, back in the day.

Me? I party.

Planet 365/Ellismania.com – Photographer Juliet Lowrie

Rob "Sluggo" Boyce

Being fit makes you want to take your shirt off.

Mike Blabac

With UFC bantamweight champion Dominick Cruz. It blows my mind that a fighter of such legendary status will be seen standing next to me.

Jayson Steele Fox

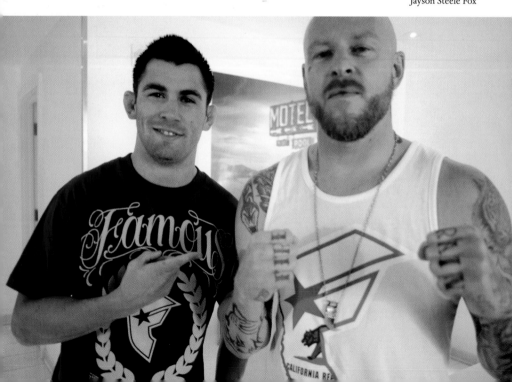

On my way to the ring to box former UFC fighter Gabe Ruediger at Ellismania 9. As always, my look is completely on point.

Jayson Steele Fox

Celebrating a knockout victory over Gabe.

Planet 365/Ellismania.com

– Videography Planet 365

This is how you party: with my good friends Rob "Sluggo" Boyce and Colin McKay of the Red Dragons, in a hotel room with its own private bowling alley at the Hard Rock Hotel in Las Vegas.

Rob "Sluggo" Boyce

The future of radio, ruling the airwaves.

Ryan Steely / www.ryansteely.com

A (fake) tattoo of Malin Akerman, on the set of the TV show *Children's Hospital*. Later on, Malin came by my radio show and gave me a real tattoo—her name on my ass cheek.

Courtesy of the author

My daughter, Devin, the flower girl at my wedding and the love of my life.

Rob "Sluggo" Boyce

Introducing my son, Tiger, to one of his relatives.

Courtesy of the author

Getting a head tattoo is like choosing to wear the same T-shirt for the rest of your life. Only it's on your head. So you better choose carefully.

Mike Blabac

vigorous finger-bang is a very amateur thing. At this point in the twenty-first century, it's just disrespectful.

And there's no need for it. The cookie wiggle is what really gets them anyway. By "cookie wiggle," I mean that you have to use your fingers to massage the clitoris. (I think we can all agree that "cookie wiggle" sounds a lot friendlier than "massage the clitoris.") To properly execute the cookie wiggle, you've got to make sure you come in soft and gentle. Some chicks like it rough, but nobody likes it rough straight off the bat. So you've really got to wait. Take a very long time. Give her a couple of good spurts and then stop again. Fuck with her mind. That's what women like. (In more ways than one.)

Of course, to pull off the cookie wiggle, you also need to know where the clit is. I feel like a lot of dudes should seriously do some research into vaginas. Get videos and really look at them, because they're all different shapes. Get one of those plastic vaginas like they would have at a doctor's office. Pull it apart. Look at it. Study it. If you don't know what you're doing, you could easily find yourself sucking away on the wrong bit. To women, that makes it very obvious you have no idea what you're doing. At that point you might as well start humping her leg.

I remember the first couple times I licked a cookie. This would have been in the pre-waxing era of vaginas. I didn't want to go down there. But the bottom line is that you need to embrace performing oral sex as early in your career as possible. If you're a young guy, maybe you don't really like it, but you're doing it to build up to something else. Or you're doing it because you want to tell your friends about it later. I understand. That's the way it is when you start.

But you need to get over that. I've gotten blow jobs from porn stars who have literally won awards for their oral skills. And yet the truly best blow jobs I've ever had were from girls who genuinely love sucking dick. And that works both ways. The guy who really loves licking girls is the guy who's good at it. If you're doing it because you feel obligated, then honestly, on behalf of women, don't even bother.

Just like most things guys do wrong in bed, when it comes to actual sex, the biggest mistake dudes make is going in too soon and too hard. You need to feel your way in there. A little bit in, and then a little bit back out. Take your time. No drastic moves. Look at it this way—there's a good chance the girl made you run the gauntlet to get this far. Now that you're home free, why not take the opportunity to fuck with her a little bit?

If you get too excited and start jackhammering away, you run the risk of prematurely blowing your load. If you're a dude who shoots his load too fast, there's simple a way to fix that. You just have to do that tantric bullshit that Sting is famous for. It's not complicated. You jerk off, and almost come, and then stop. And then you just keep doing that over and over again. Every night you practice, and then you get some control over your premature load.

If premature ejaculation happens, you can apologize. You can try to say that it only happened because she's so ridiculously hot that you lost all power over your urethra. Depending on the girl, she may never want to speak to you ever again. But I guess you would still have a chance to bounce back. As soon as you're finished making fun of yourself for being so terrible in bed, you should immediately go down on her. By doing that, you buy some recovery time while you try to mount a comeback. But remember, it doesn't need to come to that. Just slow the fuck down.

At this point, let me remind guys why I believe you should be doing some serious grooming of your penis, balls, and ass area. If you want to have sex from every possible angle and to use your genitals in all the ways that God intended, you need to be groomed. For one thing, you're not going to be able to shower before every single time you have sex. If your ass is hairy, and you used the bathroom that day and just cleaned up with toilet paper, then you are not 100 percent clean. Mix your shitty ass with a vigorous sweat, and you are officially disgusting. You may not agree with me. Personally, I think it's wild that I even have to explain this to people.

I know people will tell you that some women like a hairy man. I'm sure that's true, but I'm also sure that those women aren't having sex at an elite level. When a girl says she likes hairy men, that tells me that she just likes getting pounded by a big bear in the missionary position. That is not a frisky woman. She probably doesn't even give blow jobs.

Once you're having sex—taking care that you're alternating the speed and severity of your pumps and not just thrusting away like an idiot—you might want to mix in a little dirty talk. I don't have any set lines that I use in bed. Knowing what to say comes down to reading your partner and reading the situation. I have a radio show where I deal with people all day. If I have one talent, it's the ability to roll with people and to figure out how to talk to them. I'm not sure it can be taught.

But I can give you some guidelines. I don't think you should say anything that's really long. You wanna keep it brief and to the point. "Fuck" is a good all-purpose word. But I would lay off "cunt" until things have really escalated to somewhere well beyond normal, everyday banging. When it comes to talking dirty, if you feel like something is too risky to say out loud, then I'd play it safe and skip it. You can blow the whole night by dropping an uncalled-for C-bomb, and that's a risk you don't need to be taking.

Of course, if the girl says something crazy, don't question it. Try not to worry about whether you might have your penis inside of an insane person who is going to murder you when you sleep, and just keep going.

By now, I think everyone knows that some girls will fake orgasms. Girls on the show have told me they do it. If any of you ladies out there are not being sufficiently satisfied by your dude, I don't think you should fake it. I feel like you should tell him what's up and then try to help him fix it.

Although truthfully, I don't think it's that hard to tell when a girl is faking. The only reason guys don't notice is because some guys don't actually care if a girl gets off or not. They're just trying to fuck chicks for their own gratification and then go home and brag to their buddies. Personally, I sleep with a lot of girls, and I can pretty much guarantee no one who's having sex with me has to fake anything. That's because I genuinely like the people I sleep with. I pay attention to them, and I try to hook them up at least as much as they're hooking me up. It's not that difficult. I also care about figuring out what my partner is into. I figure that if she's happy, she's going to make me happy. And then everybody wins.

One of the questions I hear all the time on my radio show is "How do I get my chick to have anal sex?" Because of the Internet and TV and, well, things like my radio show, a lot of guys have the idea that tons of girls are taking it up the ass. These guys figure that if their wife or girlfriend isn't begging to get ass-fucked on a nightly basis, then they're getting cheated and missing out.

But I think you'll find that most girls don't really enjoy anal. And if they do, you won't have to ask or beg. They'll let you know. When it comes to ass play, asking a girl to do it is your first mistake. If you're interested in getting more friendly with a particular butthole, assuming you know it's clean, just get down there and lick it for a while. After that, gently insert just a pinkie, and not even all the way. Then see how she reacts. If she arches her back, that's good. You might be onto something. But more than anything, the butt itself will tell you if you should try going any farther.

If you have your pinkie in and you're not sure what the ass is telling you, then that's probably a no. If she wants to give you the go-ahead, it will already be open in a way. Asses are different for girls who like to get fucked there. They want to let it in. If you can get two fingers in and she's clearly enjoying it, then I like your chances of completing the rest of your mission.

Girls who get off on anal sex get completely different orgasms from it. Maybe they don't do it all the time, but from time to time they love a good ass fucking because of that special orgasm they get. And it's not messy with experienced girls, because they know what they're doing.

Don't get me wrong, some girls probably do learn to enjoy anal sex by trying it a couple different times. If your wife or girlfriend isn't sure but she's willing to give it a go, then by all means take her up on it. But if your chick tries anal and doesn't like it, or if she doesn't want to try it in the first place, then you need to let it go. If you really need to fuck somebody in the ass to be happy, then you need to leave your girlfriend and find a chick who's into it. If you think she's just humoring you or just trying to make you happy, then take my advice and nip it in the bud. Because nine times out of ten it won't end well. If you're not sure if she really wants it, then sorry—she doesn't want it.

If you're looking to spice things up, you might be thinking about occasionally moving sex out of your house and into public spaces. There's really only one rule for having sex in public: Don't get caught. You could get in big trouble for that shit.

Doing it at night is the best, because nobody can really see you. You know you're out there, and that's what's important. Obviously, you don't want to have sex in a really public place, like where kids might see you. If you live near the beach, I would also recommend having sex in the water. (Don't forget the waterproof lube.) Somebody's really going to have to go out of their way to stare you down and figure out what you're doing. That guy's going to know, but so what? Congratulations to that guy.

Balconies are also good. Ideally, if you're going to have sex outside, you should find a place where you can see people coming. Going to jail for fucking in public might be a great story ten years down the road. But I guarantee you your chick is not going to see it that way that night, when both of you are in a holding cell.

I also love fucking in cars. But getting blow jobs and driving is really dangerous. When it comes to sex in cars, you've got to know yourself. Are you a guy who can come and still handle pedals and see oncoming traffic? Or are you a guy who could potentially murder the whole freeway if a sneeze sneaks up on you? You've got to be honest with yourself, before you kill us all.

I definitely don't recommend having actual sex while you're driving. Even if you're a really good driver, that's still really dangerous. And if things get critical, there's no way she has a seat belt on. I'm not saying I've never done it. I'm just saying that when I did, I was not being very responsible. I was not in my best evasive-maneuver position.

The first level up from regular sex is threesomes. There are two kinds of those. There's the kind where you tell your girlfriend you want to bring another chick into the mix. We'll deal with that in another chapter, when we talk about all the other stupid things people do to ruin their relationships. Right now, we're talking about the other kind, when you get to fuck two drunk chicks at the same time. (Obviously, there's also the kind you have with a chick and a dude, but you can read someone else's book to find out the right way to do that.)

Naturally, the two chicks don't have to be drunk. And if they're sloppy and don't know what they're doing, it goes without saying you shouldn't take advantage of anyone. But in my experience, if you have a chance to have sex with two women at the same time, and you're not already in a relationship with one of them, the odds are approximately 100 percent that both of them will have been drinking.

Everyone wants to know how to land a threesome. I wish I could tell you the big secret, but a lot of times, just like spontaneous sex with strangers, getting a threesome comes down to luck. These girls were going to fuck somebody that night and you stumbled into it. The first time I had sex with two girls that I didn't know beforehand, it was with these two Italian chicks I met in San Diego. We were all young, and they were hot and kind of buzzed. I think all three of us were just trying to have some adventures while we were in America.

I chatted them up until they took me back to their apartment. They both started making out with me, and then things went from there. They were the ones in the driver's seat. And they had hairy armpits. I don't remember the sex being that spectacular. But hey— threesome with two horny Italian women! We've all done worse.

If the girls aren't just random strangers, for two chicks to fuck you at the same time, probably one of them is really into you, and she's convinced her friend to take one for the team. Sometimes girls will do that, especially when they're younger. In my experience, young girls are more open to crazy experiences. The older girls get, the less chance that threesomes will happen. Once they're older, they've usually decided that if a guy is not totally into them and only them, then they don't want anything to do with him.

I should mention that cocaine can also help threesomes happen. I don't really advocate using cocaine, but, as I told you in the last chapter, coke whores don't give a shit. Get some rails under them, and they'll totally lick each other's boxes, even if they're not bisexual when they're sober.

Anyway, the most important thing a man needs to know about threesomes is that they're hard work. You have to please two women, and you only have one dick. The girls might make out with each other, but—assuming there's no cocaine involved—they won't lick each other. So it's your responsibility to keep them both riled up. If you neglect one of them for as much as ten seconds, there's a good chance she'll walk out. If you bang one of them a little too much, the other one might leave. You have to work both of them up to fucking at the same time. Chicks hate feeling left out. If you're not on top of your game, your threesome could be over before it starts.

If you're going to try to please two women at one time, you might be considering taking a boner pill. I strongly recommend against that. If you have a medical condition, then of course it's okay. But if you don't need them, don't take them. You can do permanent damage to your dick, for no reason.

I had a threesome one time in Philadelphia. The girls knew who I was because at that time I was on TV with *Tony Hawk's Gigantic Skatepark Tour*. I'm definitely not going to lie. Being on TV makes pulling threesomes a lot easier. But you still have to do the work. Both of these girls thought I was cute, and I believe both of them were trying to hook up with me. So I took them back to the hotel room and then got to work. As soon as they agreed and the clothes started to come off, if one was on my dick, I made sure the other was on my mouth. Or I had both my hands in the front of their pants, and I made out with both of them, back and forth. I would switch from one to the other really quickly, not spending too long with either of them. You cannot just let one sit.

A small tip, by the way: If you're making out with one chick while you're fucking the other one, hold on to the head of the one you're kissing. Otherwise, you're going to smash each other's teeth, guaranteed.

Don't forget, once you start banging two chicks at the same time, you need to hold out twice as long. You need to make both of them come. And if anybody wants to do it again, then you need to give it to them again. You need to hold out until everyone is satisfied. Threesomes require stamina. You might want to pack some Pedialyte.

Sometimes, girls regret threesomes as soon as they're over— basically because a couple of friends just watched each other fuck some dude. Things can get weird. But if threesomes stay in the bed with you overnight, well, that's awesome, because that means you're fucking them again in the morning. By the time you wake up, you've already won. You had sex with two chicks all night, and the fact that they're still there means they're both still happy. The key for you is to try to wake up before them and immediately start licking and fingering people. Keep that party going as long as possible.

STDs are not a very sexy topic, which is why I've saved them for the end of this chapter.

I know there are guys out there who choose to not wear condoms. It fucking blows my mind, but I know it's true. We all know it feels better to go raw dog, but . . . come on. It's a dangerous world out there. So many people have so many things.

If you need me to put the fear in you, then let me tell you about the time I got syphilis. My dick had a red rash all over it, and yes, there was some discharge. I also felt sick to my stomach. They can cure syphilis, so it did go away. But the worst part was when the doctor told me they were putting me on the list of people in California who have had syphilis. I'm not even sure what the official reason is for keeping the list. I assume it's because they want to know where all the dirty disgusting whores are. That's what I took away from that phone call, anyway.

You may be reading this and thinking your no-condom-wearing ass could never get something as bad as syphilis. But tons of people nowadays have herpes, and they don't even have a cure for that. And don't think that isn't going to cramp your style. If you thought it was hard to get laid before, now it's going to be twice as hard. When you meet a girl, you're going to have to tell her what's up and then cross your fingers and hope she has herpes, too. Or else you're fucked.

And yes, if you have herpes, you do absolutely have to tell people before they sleep with you. Secretly spreading herpes is pure evil.

6

HOW TO GET LAID (ADVANCED LEVEL)

A LOT OF PEOPLE'S SEX lives will probably be limited to having normal sex with normal chicks. Guy meets girl, guy fucks girl, and that's about it. Missionary, doggy style, maybe anal on your birthday. Perhaps the odd threesome. If that's all you want—or that's all you can get—then for most people that will be fine.

But since you read that last chapter and are now a master of sex, perhaps you want to push the limits a bit. There's a whole world of creepier and more elaborate encounters waiting for you out there. In this chapter, we'll cover some next-level shit, like having group sex, paying for sex, and taking a stripper home from the club.

Like with a lot of things in this book, I'm not saying you need to go out and do all this stuff. If you're not that kind of guy, you shouldn't pretend that you are. But if you're looking to take things to the next level, then you can probably benefit from my experience.

After threesomes, the next frontier would be orgies.

Above all, orgies require a lot of women. If there's one woman or two women and then there are half a dozen dudes, personally I'm not into it. There aren't enough lady parts to go around, and sooner or later, somebody's going to grab your dick. If that happens to you, you're not allowed to punch the guy. If you weren't prepared for that to happen, you shouldn't have been there in the first place. You just have to say no thanks and then put your pants on and leave.

In my experience, there is never a shortage of dicks at orgies. So if you don't have a girl with you, then you're not invited. If you happen to encounter a group of horny naked women who can't rustle up enough penises to go around, then congratulations, you are The Man. But in my travels, I've never stumbled onto that one.

There are two kinds of orgies: the ones that just happen and the ones you arrange beforehand. Generally speaking, unplanned orgies break out when there are too many drugs at a party. Somebody—and by somebody, I mean a girl—gets naked and starts fucking someone. And then she leans over and pulls a dick out of another guy's pants. As soon that happens, it's game on. You can safely assume that anybody who didn't leave the room when the chick started blowing two dudes would like to join in.

One of the small drawbacks of unplanned orgies is that hideous people may be involved. While you're banging someone, you may have nasty strangers bumping into you. Try not to let that ruin your night. It goes with the territory. Ugly people are just part of the scenery. Focus on the bright side, which is that you're taking part in an orgy.

These kinds of orgies can sometimes get pretty risky. Someone can stick their dick in a chick without her permission. I've seen it a million times. She's blowing somebody and some other dude figures he can just slide it in from behind because hey, it's an orgy. What's one more dick going to be? But that shit is unacceptable. Sometimes, on the way in, the guy may give her a little tap as a heads-up, like, "Hey, here I come!" But maybe she's distracted by blowing some guy, and she doesn't realize he's coming in hot. Usually, the girl will turn around and inform the dude to get the fuck out of her. And then that guy's out. Don't stick your dick in anybody without permission, or else no orgy for you, and probably no more party, either.

If you're talking about a planned orgy, then you're talking about swinging. I haven't done a ton of swinging, but I've seen enough to basically know what I'm talking about. Planned orgies are the best kind, in my experience. Usually, you and your girlfriend have a couple that you swap with, and then they invite some of their friends. Everybody knows each other. Everybody's agreed to it beforehand. You can just sprawl out naked and get comfortable. Plus, you know there's no AIDS or herpes in the room, which goes a long way toward creating a more casual orgy environment.

Big swinger parties are a different story. Now you're talking about a bunch of strangers. I've only been to one of those. My girlfriend found out about it on the Internet, so we went to check it out.

The first thing about swinger parties is that you need to be comfortable with yourself naked. When you walk in, you're the only person in the room with clothes on. Everybody there will already be naked. And then you're going to walk around naked, too. You're not going to be showing your best angle all the time. You may have to bend over for some reason. I'm a fucking show pony, and I don't think I look bad in the nude, but that was still a pretty nerve-racking experience for me. You need to be able to handle some pressure, knowing that every time you walk through a room, forty people are all checking out your dick.

When it comes to swapping partners with another couple at a swinger party, the first thing I would do is size up the dude. Do you want him anywhere near your chick? Do you want him anywhere near you? If the answer is no, then I don't care how hot his girl is. No deal.

There will definitely be some oddballs at a swinger party, and there will also be some dirty motherfuckers. I don't care how old they are or how intelligent they seem or how successful they may be in their professional lives. Even if he's a CEO and she's an astronaut, they're also swingers, and that means that everyone needs to wear a rubber.

So far, we're just talking about people in the amateur ranks of sex. The next realm to consider is the professionals.

Let me again be clear: No one is saying you need to have sex with strippers and prostitutes. You could definitely make the argument that you're better off skipping them both and just getting a girlfriend instead. If you want to fuck strippers and hookers, you will most likely be signing up for some bad times. You may end up seeing some creepy shit.

But if you think you're that kind of guy, then let me lay down some ground rules.

We'll kick things off with strippers. I have known more than a few strippers over the years. I dated a stripper for years in Australia, and then after we broke up I immediately married her best friend, who was also a stripper. Years later, I also went out with a series of strippers from Vegas, including one who purred like a kitten in public, danced in 50 Cent videos, and enjoyed getting choked out during sex to the point of unconsciousness.

Picking up a stripper isn't easy. It can take some time and some effort. Here's how I've learned to pull it off, step by step.

Daytime is a good window to try your luck at a strip club. It's slow during the day, so the girls are usually bored shitless. If you hang out, buy some dances, have a couple drinks with them, and maybe make them laugh a little, that's going to go a long way.

Picking up a stripper is basically a gigantic game of lies. Strippers make their money by lying. They're like car salesmen, only they sell their vaginas. (The other difference is that no one gets to keep the car—everyone's just renting.) If by chance things work out between you and a stripper, and you end up dating her, later on you can tell her the truth about yourself. No stripper is ever going to get mad at you for telling a bunch of lies when you met just so you could fuck her. She lies all day to get your money, so it's a fair trade. It's like honor among thieves.

But when you first go to the strip club, you are going to lie your ass off. Specifically, you are going to pretend you're rich, because strippers like money. If you've got a chain on, make sure it's real. Some strippers might not be that smart, but they can all spot fake gold. You're basically dealing with drug dealers with tits. They'll know if you're rocking a cubic zirconia. So only have real ice or don't have it at all. Fake jewelry is the biggest possible turn-off for strippers, because they know that means you're a liar—and, even worse, that you're broke.

You also need to be extremely assertive. Whatever the question is, commit to your answer completely. If she asks you if you want a dance and you say, "Hmm, let me think about it," then she starts to think maybe you don't have enough money. If you don't want a dance, that's fine. Say, "No, thank you," and then she'll leave. But if you do want a dance, don't think—just say yes.

She might also ask if you want that dance in the champagne room. If you want to have a chance at sleeping with her, you have to say yes to that, too. When she tells you how much it costs to go to the champagne room, make it clear that you don't care about the price—even if you can barely afford it. If anything, you need to act like it's kind of annoying she even brought it up, because obviously money is no object to you. Look at it this way: When you order a coffee at Starbucks, do you ask how much it costs? No, because no matter how much it is, you know you have more than enough in your pocket. That's how you need to act when it comes to paying for dances. Remember, it's all a lie. You're playing a part.

Naturally it helps if you're good-looking. Strippers generally don't fuck ugly people. If you've got some style and you talk a mean game, you might be able to overcome an ugly problem. Just don't become one of those idiots who go to the club and work on the same girl for a year. That's how strippers make their money, off of regulars. Most regulars don't get lap dances. They just talk to the girls. But they hand out more money than the guys who do get dances. And the stripper takes her regular's money, pays her rent, and then goes and fucks someone else. I will repeat: Do not be that goober.

Strippers also don't fuck guys with little dicks. Although from what I've heard, even girls who don't strip can be a little bit mean about small penises. Obviously I can't speak from experience here, since my dick is humongous. But some girls have told me that if a penis is too small, they will literally take their hand out of a guy's pants and leave. Ladies, if you're reading this right now and that has ever applied to you, you should be ashamed of yourself. I have seen some scary-looking naked people in my day, and never once has that stopped me from getting the job done.

When it comes to strippers, they size up what you're packing during the lap dance. While they're giving you the dance, they get you hard, and then they feel to see if your dick is big enough. If it's not, again, I hope you are an amazing conversationalist. But don't get me wrong—it doesn't have to be huge. Average is okay. Despite what you might think, it's not all giant gaping vaginas in strip clubs.

Whatever kind of dick you're slinging, you want to make sure you smell good when she's grinding on you. It also helps a lot if you're in shape. Strippers always try to feel your stomach. When her hand moves in that direction, be ready for it. Try to be as hard-bodied and flat as you can in that moment. Tense up, if necessary. Do what you've got to do.

By now, hopefully you've got a little conversation going with your stripper of choice. So what do you talk about? Believe it or not, compliments are dangerous. You might think it's a no-brainer to say, "Hey, I think you're really beautiful." But if you do that, you're fucked. That's a really mushy thing to say in a strip club. If you want to tell her she's hot when you first meet her, that might be okay. But if you've been talking for a while and she's already given you a dance, throwing out big compliments gives strippers power that you don't want them to have.

You don't want to seem like you're in awe. You want to have confidence, even if it's fake confidence. Otherwise you seem desperate. There have been times that I've been talking to really hot strippers, and I couldn't handle it, so I panicked and played the mushy card.

And when that happened, I always blew it. I don't think it was because the girl was necessarily out of my league. It was because I lost my composure. When I go to a club and make it obvious that I don't care one way or another if I have sex with a stripper, that's usually when one of them wants to fuck me.

Here's an example: Recently, I had some time to kill so I stopped in a club. Two girls wanted to dance for me. I only wanted one, but I didn't hesitate. I just said yes. Then they asked me if I wanted to go into the champagne room. I didn't really feel like spending the money, but I didn't ask how much it was or try to get rid of the second girl. I knew that wasn't going to work. Once again, I just said yes to both of them, immediately.

After we went in there, they were dancing for me, and then one of them started putting her hands in my pants. But at this particular point in time, I had a scab on my dick. (It's not what you're thinking. I had recently been dry-humping this other chick for like an hour and rubbing my dick on my zipper the whole time. The scab was the ugly reminder of that marathon blue-balling session. I blame the girl. I mean, who the fuck dry-humps anymore? I'm forty!) When the stripper started putting her hand in my boxers, I pushed it away. I was like, "We don't know each other like that." Naturally, she loved it. Because every guy in the world wants her hand down there. I got her phone number in like three seconds.

You want to surprise a stripper. Say something that has shock value. Don't confess to a triple homicide or anything too over-the-top—just say something she wouldn't expect a man to admit. Lie if you have to. If you don't have any secrets, make one up. Tell her you're an art thief. Or tell her you once had a gay encounter. I did that once, accidentally. I was talking to a stripper, and I couldn't hear a question she was asking me, but for some reason I just said yes.

She looked surprised. She was like, "You fuck guys?"

I have no idea how the conversation had evolved to that point, but I just went with it. "From time to time. Sure. What's the big deal?"

She jumped on that. "You do?" Now she was interested, because all of a sudden I wasn't just another dude saying the same old bullshit. No, now I was apparently a raging bisexual. But hey, it worked.

Being a bad boy works, too. Being all the things guys shouldn't be is a turn-on to a lot of strippers. I figured that out when I was young. Back then, I wasn't trying to be a bad boy. But I was a self-centered egomaniac. (And you think I'm bad now.) I wasn't listening to what other people had to say. If a stripper was talking to me, I wasn't really paying attention. And I think they liked that. I'm not trying be mean—I'm just telling you how it seemed to me. I never paid attention to them and they loved it. Or they hated it. Or a little bit of both. Whatever you want to call their reaction, clearly they responded to it.

Once you've got a stripper who's willing to talk to you, don't leave the club. You've got her on the hook, and if you go somewhere else, you're fucked. But you don't have to give her money to talk to you. Just buy her drinks, keep it social, and act cool when she goes and dances for other people.

One word of warning: If you think you have a chance with your stripper, don't get a dance off of another girl. Don't even be nice to any of the other girls. Because strippers hate each other.

You'll have to wait until closing time to go home with her. Strippers aren't allowed to fuck clients, so usually you meet them in the parking lot, or down the street if they think their boss is watching. Sometimes she might tell you to meet her in the parking lot and then never come out. Obviously in that case you're fucked. But if she meets you outside the club, then congratulations, it's officially on.

If you're going home with someone from a strip club, she's going to be pretty buzzed. I don't think I've ever had sex with a stripper who wasn't drunk when I picked her up after work. I think they drink all night to help them dance. A lot of them might also pop a Xanax or an Oxy to go with their Chardonnays, too. That's just the stripper world. They all like taking the edge off. It's got to be a hard job, showing creepy guys your hole all night.

Once you get her out of the club, treat her like a lady. I find that keeps strippers on their toes. Don't worry, things will get plenty loose once you get home. Almost every stripper I've ever fucked loved rough sex—getting choked out, getting her hair pulled, getting slapped, all that good stuff.

If you have a shitty house, then go to her place. Back in my stripper-fucking heyday, most of the time I had roommates, so I would always try to take the party to her house. Usually they either live by themselves or they live with another stripper. If that's the case, your night could turn out very fucking awesome. Very rarely has that dream scenario played out, but yes, it has happened. Some strippers do like to share.

One of my stripper girlfriends had this blond-haired friend who was very hot and super gay. I once spent a week sleeping in bed with the both of them. I remember I plucked their eyebrows, and they liked the job I did so much they brought over all the other strippers from the club so I could pluck their eyebrows, too. Although I think the other chicks really just wanted to put their heads on my lap so they could fuck with my penis's emotions.

Over the course of your late night with a stripper, if it turns out that she's really annoying, or she's bad in bed, then it's probably better if either you or her is gone by daylight. That's one of the good things about going to her house. Then you can leave. Tell her you've got to work in the morning, even if you don't have a job. No one can argue with that one.

Any time I took a stripper back to my house and then decided I had to get rid of her, I would make someone call me and pretend to be my boss. (Well, not always, because I'm a sucker. But the times I was smart I did.) I would text a friend, tell them to call me, and then tell the chick I had to go do something. Sometimes they probably knew it was bullshit, but they still left. And that's all you want. Whether she figures it out or not, it's more polite than the alternative. If you're trying to get someone you recently had sex with out the door, I don't think saying "Fuck off" is a very nice way to do it.

And make no mistake, letting a stripper hang around is just asking for trouble. I've had relationships with numerous strippers, but never one that I met at a club while she was working. You're talking about someone who was drinking and dancing and maybe popping pills all night, and then went home with some random dude who gave her a hundred dollars. That's a potentially suspect individual.

A lot of things can go wrong if a crazy stripper starts thinking a little relationship might be brewing. They might stalk you and then block you from other chicks, especially now that there's Twitter and all that other bullshit. If there's a picture of you and another girl online, she might post some stuff. "Just so you know, I fucked him last night." Shit like that. I know, it's hard to believe, but if you don't play your cards right, you could end up paying a price for fucking a stripper.

Although, on the flip side, if you fuck one of the chicks at a strip club and then you don't keep seeing her afterward, don't think you can never go back to that club again. They don't care. It's mellow.

The stripper you hooked up with might try to ruin things for you with the rest of them, but that's about as bad as it's going to get. Put it this way: I've never fucked every girl in the same club. But any place I ever fucked a stripper, I always ended up fucking more than one.

The bottom line is, if you succeed in picking up a stripper, you may well have an awesome time. Just remember that you are signing up for a wild ride. And you may not be in the driver's seat.

Let me give you an idea of what you might be dealing with: I met a girl one time. I think it was in Philadelphia. She was the craziest bitch in the whole club, and I do mean both "craziest" and "bitch" in the most complimentary way possible. She was jumping off stuff and landing in full splits. She had a gift.

I hit on her and got her number, and then later that night I met her outside the club. First she took me back to her apartment, which was a rowdy-looking place. I remember she had a massive pit bull. And she led me into her bedroom, where she reached under the bed and pulled out a shotgun. She then proceeded to empty the bullets onto her bed and put the gun back away. Then she said, "Okay, we can go now." There was no further explanation, and I didn't ask. In retrospect, obviously she just wanted to show me that she owned a high-caliber weapon.

Then we went back to my hotel room. I was trying to put some porn on the TV when suddenly she attacked me. She grabbed my shirt and tried to tear it off me. She didn't get my wife-beater off, but she did manage to use it to throw me to the ground. Then she pounced on top of me and punched me in the head.

I thought she was robbing me. (Or trying to rob me. I mean, I wasn't about to beat up a girl, but I can take a stripper pretty easily.)

But then I saw the look on her face.

That's when I realized this was how she made love.

I was younger then and hadn't seen as many things as I have now. This was the first time in my life I got scratched all over, really hard. I was young and drunk and really horny, so I went with it. But I would not say that I liked it. I remember her kicking me repeatedly and yelling insults about my Australian heritage, all in between fucking me.

The next night, I went back to the same club with Ken Block, who was then the head of DC Shoes and who is now obnoxiously famous for making drift car videos. (This was before Ken was married. It goes without saying that nowadays he finds the idea of strip clubs completely repulsive.) And the chick comes over and sits on my lap. Because obviously, in her mind we were now boyfriend and girlfriend. Two peas in a pod. Ken quickly sized up this motley bitch and then gave me a look like, "What is wrong with you?" I say, what's wrong with him? You only live once. Me and that girl ended up hanging out together for like a week. We got pedicures together. She was kind of cool. You know, except for the parts of her that were not cool in the slightest. When it comes to strippers, you have to take the good with the bad.

That brings us to prostitutes. Prostitutes are a different animal entirely.

One rule applies to all prostitutes, across the board: If they ask you if you're a police officer, don't make a joke about it. If you do, you've just ruined your night. If you so much as stutter-step on the answer, you could easily fuck yourself out of a BJ.

There are several different kinds of prostitutes I came across during my illustrious career of paying for sex.

First you have your top-of-the-line hookers. They charge $1,000 an hour, $15,000 for the night. Yes, they're really out there. They look just like supermodels, only usually they were too lazy to put the work in to make it in modeling. Somewhere along the line they decided they'd rather just have sex with old billionaires for a living. I have personally never fucked any prostitutes on this level, but I've hung out with some of them at gyms around Hollywood. That's how I got the scoop.

They're mainly there so an old rich guy can take them to restaurants and make everyone think they're his girlfriend. It's the same reason a guy like that buys a Lamborghini—so people can see him driving it up and down Sunset Boulevard all day. It's mainly a status symbol.

If you want to hang out with hot chicks because you think it makes you look cool, I would recommend you just pretend you're gay. Then you can get hot girls to hang out with you, no problem. Because even if I had fifteen grand to blow on a night with a hooker, I feel like the purpose of prostitution is to have really fun sex. And these girls are really, really hot, but my gut tells me that a night with a top-of-the-line prostitute ends with some pretty average fucking.

As a general rule, most really hot girls are nothing special in bed. I've never fucked an amazingly hot chick who had anything out of the ordinary to offer me sexually, other than the fact that I got to keep looking at her and thinking about how hot she is. In terms of actual moves, there's never much going on.

It's kind of a cliché, but a lot of hot chicks suck in bed for the same reason a lot of them don't have amazing personalities—because they can get away with it. I feel like it's gross to say that fat girls suck dick better, but there's a little bit of truth to that. It's not that all fat girls kick ass at giving blow jobs. But if a girl isn't mind-blowing to look at, there's a better chance she'll develop some charisma, or at least put in some effort when you're in bed. Hot chicks—and hot prostitutes—coast on their looks. It's just human nature.

Most guys will never spend a thousand dollars for sex. Most guys who want to have sex with prostitutes probably wind up at brothels. If you go to a brothel, you only have to pay about $300, and you know you won't get any diseases, because all the girls there get tested. But on the other hand, the girls there have to work all night. And personally, I don't like the idea of putting my penis inside a woman who would prefer that I just leave her poor vagina alone. I don't feel like anyone wins in that situation.

I used to enjoy a good old-fashioned call girl. When things work out with one of those, it can be a good time. A girl would come to my house, and for $300 she'd have sex with me and dyke out with my chick, even if the hooker wasn't gay in the slightest. But most times it's really $300 to show up, and then they just string you along—$100 more for this, another $100 for that. You basically have to come as fast as you can, before you go bankrupt. And they're usually accompanied by a huge dude, and they inform you that if you don't give them enough money, the guy out front is going to punch you in the face.

There's also the element of mystery. When you find a girl online or in the phone book, you never know what she's going to look like. Even if it's a thousand bucks just for her to show up, she might be hot and she might not. You won't find out until she gets there, and you've got to pay her either way, unless you want the big guy to assault you.

If you read my last book, or if you listen to my radio show, then I don't need to tell you that you should generally avoid junkie street hookers. That is, unless you want to get some crazy disease or, better yet, get robbed and then left for dead in a park somewhere.

I don't generally recommend prostitutes these days, but there is one exception. If you're a virgin and you're finding it hard to get laid, you might be thinking about going to a prostitute to get the first time out of the way. If you want my opinion, I say go for it. I don't think there's anything wrong or weird about that. Hookers are nice people. I've got friends who are hookers. It doesn't make you a loser. Having sex with a prostitute doesn't automatically stick you lower on the totem pole of fuckability.

And besides, no matter who you have sex with your first time, it's not going to be that good. You're not going to blow anyone's mind. It probably won't be mind-blowing for you, either. Sex takes practice. There's a little less pressure every time.

If you're in this situation, you definitely want to tell the girl it's your first time. She's probably going to know anyway. And more importantly, don't waste that scenario. If I could get a hooker to believe that I'm a virgin, I would be in a brothel right now, because that would be the greatest sex of my life. Hookers will teach you shit. Hookers have moves, especially if you're a rookie. If you tell a prostitute that you're a virgin, unless she's a blacked-out junkie, she's going to nurture you. She'll want to baby you along and show you how to do it right.

There is a mother inside every woman—even hookers.

(Just make sure you wear a rubber.)

7

HOW TO BE A BOYFRIEND

NOW THAT YOU'VE BEEN GETTING around out there and having more mind-blowing sex than your poor overworked penis can possibly handle, you might start thinking it's time to mellow out a bit and get a girlfriend.

I have been in a ton of relationships over the years. I would like to say that some were good and some were bad. But really, they were all bad—some of the times I was just matched up with good people. Being in a relationship with me is an emotional roller coaster. There are very high highs and very low lows. I would like to think the girls I've been in extended relationships with might have found themselves a little bit as a result of being with me. Maybe they were going to do that anyway. But I've accomplished a lot of things with my life, and I think seeing the way I get things done may have rubbed off on them. Also, I can get them Twitter followers. But that's pretty much where the benefits of dating me end.

If a relationship is what you truly want, and you think you've found the right chick, then I say go for it. But before things get too far along, ask yourself what your true motivation is. Is it because that's what your parents want? Or because that's what you see everybody doing on TV? Is it because you reached a certain age and then decided it was time to grow up and get serious?

Or maybe, has a chick that you're seeing informed you that it's time for you and her to be boyfriend and girlfriend? In general, girls are more sensible than dudes. But deep down most of them still want that fairy-tale relationship. It's like they're raised to feel that way. They meet a guy, and then they start to fall in love with him, and then, after a certain amount of time, if that guy doesn't get with the program, then that guy's an asshole. Her parents and her friends hate him. Maybe *his* parents and *his* friends think he's being a dick, too. And so the guy just goes along with it.

But you've got to be careful about doing things for other people. Even if you have good intentions, there's a huge chance that's not going to work out for anyone. You can't live your life for everybody else. That's how Ricky Martin almost ended up getting married to a woman.

In my opinion, relationships are not for everybody. Maybe you just like living by yourself. Tons of people are like that. Not everybody rolls the same way. And nobody knows you better than you.

Looking back, I wish I had spent more time by myself when I was a young guy. When you're young, that's the best window you're ever going to get to grow as a person and get to know who you really are. And I'm not talking about spending all your time trying to bro down with your dude friends or playing Nintendo for eight hours a day. I mean hanging out all by yourself and finding out what you really like and what really makes you happy.

That's the perfect time in life to think about what you want for your future and how you plan to get there. Some people might call that daydreaming, but to me it's visualization. It's mental practice. And then once you have an idea of where you're going, you have the time and the space to get to work. For example, in Hollywood everybody wants to be a screenwriter. And that's a tough job to get, because everyone thinks they can be that guy. There's a lot of competition. But it can be done. If you're eighteen years old, instead of pretending the girlfriend you're going to break up with a year from now is the love of your life, you might be better off getting to work on that screenplay. If you actually get organized, get focused, and work hard day in and day out, by the time you're twenty-eight, I bet your movie script will be pretty fucking good.

And make no mistake, if any eighteen-year-olds are reading this right now, thinking they've already found the One, I'm sorry to break it to you, but you are fucking wrong. The person you are when you're eighteen isn't the person you're going to be when you're twenty-eight. And the same goes for your chick. Talk to an old person. They'll tell you: You change all the time. Especially when you're young.

If I had known myself better when I was young, I wouldn't have fallen in love with a bunch of people I wasn't compatible with. I've been married twice, and if I ever do it again, it won't be because that's what everybody else thinks I should do.

This does not mean that I'm anti-girlfriend or anti-relationship. If you genuinely feel like you're falling for a chick, then in my opinion, you need to go for it. It doesn't make you a pussy to fall in love. It makes you a pussy to try to convince yourself that you're too much of a badass to be in love. Love is extremely valuable. Don't be afraid to take a risk. If you like a girl, tell her. If you have a chance to love someone, go after it with everything you've got. Fuck what your friends think. If things go horribly wrong, so what? Lesson learned. Go cry your eyes out and then find another chick and try it all over again.

If you meet a girl, and you get her number, and you think you might really like her, don't sit on it. Waiting three days to call somebody, or whatever the rule is supposed to be—that's bullshit. It doesn't make you seem like you're so awesomely busy or build up anticipation on her end. While you're sitting around waiting, she might be giving her number to somebody who doesn't play games.

Once you get a girl out on a date, act like a gentleman. I always open car doors and stuff like that. It may not seem like much, but girls always trip out over that stuff, and that tells me that most guys don't do it. I also pay for dinner every time. It's cool if the girl offers to pay, but you shouldn't let her. If you can't afford to take care of a girl, you can't afford to have a girlfriend. You need to be as chivalrous as possible when you're out on your dates, and then when you get home, plow her mercilessly. That is how a man should behave when he's dating.

Part of being chivalrous is also being on time when you pick a girl up. It's disrespectful to keep a lady waiting, and besides, they all think it's cute if you show up when you said you would. In general,

I think being prompt is a pretty big deal, in all parts of life. Some people might not mind if you're late, but in my experience, people who have their shit together don't like waiting on people who don't. And you should want to associate with people who have their shit together. Nowadays, I'm usually early for everything. I don't like to be rushed. If I'm rushed, I forget shit. I make mistakes. And the fewer mistakes I make, the better, so personally I try to be on time, all the time.

Any time you can flash some real skills for a girl, it's a power move. But don't go out of your way to show off. Guys usually can't wait to brag about shit, and that's the exact opposite of what you should do. If you drive a nice car, then don't slide your keys in front of her at the first opportunity. Just wait and let her see it when you come to pick her up.

Back in the day, if I ever dated a girl who didn't know that I was a pro skateboarder, I definitely didn't bring it up. She was going to find out sooner or later, and when it came up accidentally, it seemed way cooler. She'd be like, "Wait a minute, you're kind of famous?" And then I got to brush it off. "Yeah, well, kind of. Not really." They love that.

If you bring up your career and all the shit you have too soon, you're liable to come across as a desperate obnoxious prick. And you also might attract the wrong kind of woman. Feel free to try to fuck whoever you want by flossing whatever you've got to floss. But if you're talking about a potential relationship, you want to weed out the girls who might try to date you for the wrong reasons.

Some guys might think there are tons of dude skills that men need to have to impress women. You might believe that a man should know how to build a house with his bare hands or be able to put food on the table using only a bow and arrow. But, even as manly as I am, I don't think it's really like that anymore. I bought my daughter a dollhouse for her last birthday, and my girlfriend was the one who ended up putting the thing together.

I don't even think you need to know how to change a tire on the side of the road. There are people you can call to do that for you. Way back, when shit broke, it stayed broken until the man did something about it. So guys needed to have a toolbox, and they needed to know how to use all the shit inside it. But let's face it—nowadays, when things are fucked up, you just take them to the Mac store.

Of course some chicks like a guy who's a bit handy. But I think most girls really just want you to make an effort. If a girl likes you and then you attempt to change a tire and you fuck it up royally, that doesn't make you lower in her eyes. There's actually something almost cute about it to them, because you tried. (Of course, if you say, "Fuck you, I'm not changing the tire," well, then that's a little different.)

If you can cook a little bit, then you're a pimp. Making dinner for your chick is a power move. But I wouldn't pull that one out on one of your first dates. Cooking dinner for a woman is a serious thing. If you're pulling that move, you're getting close to girlfriend territory there. You don't want to lay the cheese like that too early.

The biggest mistake you can make is falling in love with a chick just because she's hot. Believe me, I know what I'm talking about. You need to resist your dick. You should look for somebody who's compatible with you. I know they say that opposites attract. But they also say that 50 percent of marriages end in divorce. The safe bet is finding someone you're similar to in as many ways as possible. Similar interests, similar likes and dislikes. Similar sex drives. That's a big one. Sex isn't everything . . . unless you're not getting any.

The relationships that work happen when you're ready for a relationship. You meet somebody who just so happens to also be ready. And someone who is totally mentally equipped to have an adult relationship. Take your time, but remember that nobody's perfect. There is no such thing as The One. I've met The One at least three or four times so far, and I'm probably not done yet.

There are several warning signs you may be dating the wrong person. You shouldn't go out with girls who always get distracted by their phone or the TV when you're talking to them. And if you catch a girl lying to you, you need to get out. That's the way she's always going to be, and you can't get seriously involved with a liar. If you meet a girl who only wants to party and fuck all the time, then by all means party with her and fuck her as much as you want. But that's not the type you want for a girlfriend. And if a girl is racist or homophobic or generally just angry and bitter toward society, then steer clear of that one. Eventually you will do something to piss her off, and she will direct that rage at you. And as I explained earlier in this book, that is the kind of woman who will mutilate your genitals while you sleep.

The girl you want to go out with may already have kids. If you start dating a girl in that situation and she immediately wants you to jump in and act like the father, I would get out of there. The mother has to be in charge of her kids. She has to be able to handle them on her own until your relationship grows to the level where you might pitch in. And I think that should take a year or two. Even if you do start taking care of the kids sometimes, don't be trying to jump in there and be Super Dad. Mommy makes the rules for her kids.

There's also a chance that the girl you like will happen to be your friend's sister. Some people will tell you that means she's off-limits, but I disagree. If you're at a point in your life where you're capable of having a serious relationship, and you think this girl might be the right one for you, then I say go right ahead. Just know that you're playing for keeps. You have to make a serious attempt to date her. Under no circumstances can you just fuck your buddy's sister. Then you're just a dick.

Most of the time you don't really decide to make a relationship official—you just wake up one day and realize you have a girlfriend. There are several ways to know when the girl you're dating has turned into the girl you're going out with. You know you're in a relationship when she doesn't thank you for dinner. You know you've got a girlfriend if you're fighting, because you really can't fight if you're not in a relationship. When you feel comfortable pissing on her in the shower as your little dude joke, you know that you're in a relationship. Shower piss attacks have always told me that me and a chick have a serious bond.

To me, pissing on each other in the shower is mellow. In my world, that's a sign of affection. But being in a relationship doesn't mean you get to stop acting like a gentleman in other areas. You should still open doors for her and all that. And no matter how long you're in a relationship, you do not have permission to rip big, loud man burps. I mean, you can't stop burping entirely. Everybody does it. But they shouldn't be loud, and you should try to cover them. Some chicks are into loud gross burps, but those are the kind of chicks who have untamed vaginas and gunts.

(You may need me to define the word "gunt." You know how girls' bellies are lower than guys'? Well, if a girl gets really sloppy and out of shape, her belly may turn into a gunt. It sticks out like it's an awning for her vagina. It's a bad look, especially if a girl has no ass. If you're a white girl with a gunt and no ass, you look like you're walking backward.)

When you're in a relationship, you definitely don't fart. Despite what a lot of people seem to think, it's not funny. Don't fart on her. Don't attempt to trick her into smelling your farts. If the bathroom smells like ass when you're done in there, don't let her go in until the coast is clear.

Under no circumstances should you ever shit in front of your girlfriend. Ever. Peeing in front of each other, however, is adorable.

Losing the freedom to fart whenever you feel like it isn't the only thing that's going to change when you get into a relationship. Your life will be altered in all kinds of ways. And that should be a good thing. If you liked everything exactly the way it was, then why did you get a girlfriend in the first place?

If you're a strip club kind of guy, you're going to have to cut that out. If she's into strip clubs and wants to go there with you, that's great. But if you're going solo, that's going to end badly. You might fuck up and do something stupid there. And even if you don't, she's going to think you are. Either way, it just doesn't work. Be a strip club guy, or be a relationship guy. You can't have both.

That brings us to the subject of jealousy. Jealousy goes both ways. I'm naturally a jealous guy, and I can tell you that it's never worked out for me. Nobody wins. Now that I'm older, I can see it. Girls aren't attracted to jealousy. And stressing out about what she's doing probably isn't changing anything. So my advice, if it's at all possible, is to not give a shit.

If you're checking her Facebook and her phone, then you're already fucked. You are creating a private hell for yourself. I promise you, if you keep searching and you look hard enough, eventually you'll find some piece of information that your mind can twist into something bad. If you strongly suspect that something is up, then don't waste any time looking. You probably won't find the dirt anyway. Girls are smarter than us. Just ask her.

On the other hand, if I know my girlfriend is going through my shit, and I know I'm not doing anything wrong, then I have a rule: I give you three chances. That's it. That's how I roll. Three fuckups, and then I'm not going out with you anymore, because you're too insecure to be my girlfriend.

I don't think couples need to synchronize all of their TV watching. There's no need to give in and pretend to give a shit about *The Bachelor*. I don't think any man should be super into television anyway. Television was really invented for women. TV is fake drama, and women love fake drama. (Man, any ladies who are reading this book are going to love me.) Men mostly just watch TV because they want to watch sports and they can't actually go to all the games and fights in person.

I definitely don't support dudes who need to be left alone to stare at the TV while the football game is on. There is no need to get that obsessed over a game that you are not associated with in any way. If she wants to get into that with you, that's different. If she wants to wear a jersey and make the nachos, that's great. But if she's not into it, you shouldn't go too overboard. I guarantee you it's not a highlight for her, watching you sit there yelling at the TV and getting fat.

If your relationship is going well, your friends may start to get on you about how much time you spend with your girlfriend. In my opinion, your friends can fuck right off. I don't think any guy has a right to tell you that you're not spending enough time with him. If things change and the two of you break up, then your friends can have you back. And if you never come back, well, that means you're married to her, and you're very, very happy, because you listened to all the excellent advice I'm giving you. You made a great decision, because you took your time and you really thought about it.

Speaking of friends, you may find that you like your girlfriend a lot, but you hate the chicks she hangs out with. If that's the case, I would consider that a little bit of a warning sign. Your girlfriend is probably a lot like her friends. After all, that's why they're friends. If her friends suck, there's a chance your chick sucks just as bad as they do, and you're just not seeing it.

If your girlfriend's best friend sucks, then there's a particularly good chance you have a problem, because best friends are probably pretty similar, deep down. But if it's just her casual friends and acquaintances that suck, then that's okay. There's a chance your girlfriend hates her casual friends just as much as you do, because girls are catty and insane like that. And besides, a couple of your buddies are probably assholes, too.

If you've been dating a chick for a while, the next logical step is to move in with each other. There's no need to rush that one. Besides, if it's going to happen, it will probably kind of happen all by itself, before you even notice what's going on. If your relationship is going well, you spend all your free time together, and go to bed together, and wake up together, day after day. Eventually you realize that one of you is paying rent on a place they haven't been to in weeks. That's when you make it official, when you've had a little trial run and you haven't started to hate each other yet.

You don't want to tell someone to move in with you and not know what it's like to live with them. Because once you say you're in, you can't decide you're out. If you say you want to slow things down, she's going to break up with you. They don't go for that shit. She knows what's up, even if you don't. You're not taking a break. You're breaking up.

For most people, being in a relationship means a life of monogamy. Getting used to the idea of only having sex with one vagina can be a scary thing for men. But I do believe monogamy is possible for everybody. I think if you really want it, you can have it. I think I could be monogamous if I wanted to be. Right now I don't, but I think there'll be a time when the madness will stop. And when it stops, it'll probably really stop, because I got it out of my system.

Until I met my girlfriend, I'd never met a girl who was legitimately okay with the shit I do—namely, having sex with tons of people, all the time. A girl may tell you it's cool if you fuck around on the side, if you really have to. She may say she can deal with it. But most of the time, she's just saying what you want to hear. She may tell you it's cool, but in the end, it doesn't usually work.

And I get it. I don't think the average human mind is really equipped to handle visions of your girlfriend or your boyfriend fucking other people. I understand that completely. And make no mistake, sometimes it brings drama into my relationship. But I'm thick-skinned, and so is my chick. We're equipped to handle it because we're a really rare breed. I don't hide anything from my girlfriend, and she's the first girlfriend that I've ever done that with. My girlfriend knows everything I do and everything I want to do, and she's fine with it. That takes a special girl.

I'm sure plenty of people who are in monogamous relationships want me to tell them how to convince their chick to have a threesome. I'll tell you everything I know—although you may not like what I have to say.

When you bring up a potential threesome to your girlfriend, everything depends on her first reaction. If it's a bad one, then I would recommend you give up. You're not going to get it. You're never going to convince her otherwise. If she says no the first time you bring it up, don't ever bring it up again. I hate to have to tell you this, but either you need to resign yourself to a relationship without threesomes or you need to break up with her.

If she says yes, but you feel like she's only saying that to make you happy, I would skip it, especially if you love her. It's just like trying to have anal sex with your chick. She has to be open to it from the start. If you need to twist her arm, that means she doesn't want to do it. And in the long run, you're going to pay for it.

And by the way, ask yourself if you're totally okay with it, too. If you start banging other chicks and you find out that your girlfriend has some lesbian tendencies that she likes to indulge, is that going to make you jealous later on? Because if it is, then my advice, once again, is to just skip it. You might find out that your chick is way kinkier than you thought, and believe it or not, you might not like that. You're opening a whole new can of worms. If both of you aren't fully on board, it's probably not worth the trouble it might bring.

Threesomes with my girlfriend didn't happen at first. And they only really happen every now and again. At first, she just told me that she likes chicks. And so I was like, well, how much do you like chicks? I jumped on it the same way any other idiot dude would if their girlfriend said she was kind of a lesbian. My chick told me that she likes chicks very, very much. And then one thing led to another.

It can be a tricky subject to bring up. In the past, the only times threesomes with girlfriends ever happened for me was when I threw it out there before we were seriously dating. Very early on, I very gently and politely got the message across that a threesome was something I would be into. I let the girl know that it was totally her decision, but that if she would do that for me, then I would be forever in her debt. (If you've had threesomes before with other women, I would probably not mention that to your new chick.)

If you and your girlfriend decide you want to bring another girl into the bedroom, it's going to be up to your chick to actually make it happen. A girl gets another girl to have a threesome. It's just impolite for a dude at a bar to go over to a girl and say, "Hey, this is my girlfriend over here. Maybe the three of us could get it on!" Your girlfriend and the new chick have to hit it off. Once the three of you are drinking and having fun, you might be able to throw a couple of jokes out there and see if anybody bites. But your girlfriend is probably going to be the one who seals the deal.

Once you get the girl to come home with you, the biggest mistake dudes make is focusing too much on the new chick. It's understandable. After all, she's new and exciting. But I made that mistake once, a long time ago, and my girlfriend at the time ended up shoving her finger up my ass. And not in a cool way. It took me like twenty years to get over that.

You want to take the exact opposite approach. You don't want to be rude to the new girl, of course, so you need to keep her involved in the game. But you mostly need to be all about your girlfriend. The new girl is your girlfriend's job. I wouldn't even be the one to put my dick inside the new chick. You're better off waiting until you're inserted into her by your girlfriend. That's the only way you can know for sure that you're in the clear.

Once you're actually having sex, you may again be tempted to completely unleash yourself on the new vagina. But you have to resist that urge. Make sure you bone your girlfriend way more than you bone the bonus feature. If you make out with the new girl, make sure you make out with your girlfriend way harder and more intensely. And if at any point your wife or girlfriend demands that you take your penis out of the other girl, you need to remove it immediately. Those two extra pumps might be fun, but later on, they *will* be considered cheating.

If the new girl in the threesome is one of your chick's friends, and not a stranger, then you also need to back off at the start and let them warm up. It's going to be a little weird for them at first. They're going to giggle and stuff. And in this situation, fucking the new chick more than you fuck your girlfriend is an even more massive mistake. Again, I would let my girlfriend handle the insertion. That way, you're not making any moves on a friend. Your girlfriend is making moves, with your dick, on her friend. You can't be too careful.

In my experience, threesomes with friends never work out. The aftermath of a threesome will probably be smoother if it's with a stranger. And if it's not, you can just get rid of her. Otherwise, your girlfriend's friend might like you, which can obviously get weird. Even worse, your chick might think you like her friend more than you like her. She might decide that you kissed her friend too passionately. There might not even be any truth to these theories, but guess what—that doesn't matter.

If the aftermath gets weird, then you're never going to get another threesome again. That's happened to me a lot. I got too giddy in the heat of the moment, and I ended up fucking myself. You need to be cool. You have to play the first threesome to help get the second one. Only then can you loosen up a little bit.

Also, the two of you need to talk about it afterward. You need to figure out the things she liked and the things she didn't. You want your chick's respect.

If she's cool with how things went down, and she gets into the threesome thing, and she's generally a confident person, then at some point you might want to upgrade to swinging.

When it comes to swingers, I feel you should try to find a couple that you really like and then stick to them. Those are the ones that can turn out okay. When you get into a long-term threesome arrangement with one girl, women can't take it. In my experience, and from what I've seen with friends of mine, eventually your chick will start wondering what's so great about the other girl. And then you're fucked.

But if you're going to repeatedly swap with another couple, you need a lot confidence in yourself and your relationship. If my girlfriend wants to invite Jim and Sheila over again, I say yeah, because I know that I love my girlfriend and she loves me. If she likes fucking Jim's dick, then congratulations to Jim. I'm cool with that, because I believe that she doesn't love Jim's dick as much as she loves my dick. If either of you doubts that, then you're in the wrong game.

But if you're both cool, then you're all set. All you need to do is make sure you take precautions so you don't get Sheila pregnant. Because if that happens, you're now having kids with your friend's wife. And that's when swinging goes bad.

Whether it's because of accidental swinging pregnancies or for some other reason, at some point you may decide that your relationship with your girlfriend is over. There's only one way to end a relationship, and that's with kindness, honor, and respect. Even if she did something that made you angry, you need to handle a breakup in the nicest way possible.

You should never raise your voice. You should never lose your cool. Think of it like you're a police officer delivering a ticket. You just have to give it to her cold, and you need to remain calm. Tell her you want things to be friendly between the two of you. Obviously, you don't want to know this chick ever again, which is why you're breaking up with her. But that's how you play it. Tell her you no longer wish to continue this relationship and you hope she can understand that.

A lot of guys want to be disrespectful when they break up with chicks. They think it's cool to tell their friends that they told their ex to fuck off. But that shit comes back to haunt you, man. I don't believe in karma, but I do believe that if you're mean when you break up with your girlfriend, it will come back to bite you somehow. You never know who she knows or who she might run into. If you both live in the same town, she could give you a bad rap. You have nothing to gain from being a dick. If you break up with her in the right way, for the right reasons, and in a calm manner, the odds of that coming back to haunt you have been minimized.

When you break up with a girl, you might tell her that she isn't the problem. But you need to remember that you're lying. You're trying to let her down nicely. If you still liked hanging out with her, then you wouldn't be breaking up. Once you let her down nicely, you need to get out of the picture. Don't drag it out.

You can't stay friends with her. Being friends with ex-girlfriends is so obviously stupid, they make sitcoms about it. If you're in the relationship game, that means you're trying to find the right person to settle down with for the rest of your life. And if you're in the getting-laid game, then you're now trying to have sex with a bunch of hot chicks.

Either way, I don't see how having your ex-girlfriend around is going to help.

8

HOW TO BE A HUSBAND

THE SINGLE BEST JOKE IN this whole book might be the fact that I am now about to give you marriage advice. I may be awesome at a lot of things, but at least so far, marriage is not one of them. Still, you don't go in and out of two marriages without learning a few things—usually the hard way. If you're thinking about getting married, I can at least tell you what not to do.

My first marriage was bad on a legendary level. I married a girl who was the cutest, most gorgeous little button of a person. And then after we got married, one day something clicked inside her brain and she became the most violent person ever. I got kicked and punched in the face. I got head-stomped. I routinely took verbal abuse. "Shut the fuck up, you dumb cunt." Stuff like that. As I have said, I am not an easy person to be in a relationship with, but nobody deserves what I put up with. It was like a bad movie.

I doubt most people reading this book will be physically abused by their wives. But make no mistake, marriage is hard. And it's harder today than it ever used to be. Think about it: When your grandparents got married, they were probably virgins. Getting married was the only way either of them could ever get laid. And there weren't all these statistics out there about how many people were cheating on each other. Don't get me wrong—people have always cheated. But back then, people didn't realize that everyone was fucking everybody else behind each other's backs. Having an affair still seemed like a big deal. And no one got divorced back then either. So once you got married, your choice was to either stick it out together or die alone in a hellish world of sad masturbation.

And there weren't celebrities on TV all the time, showing off their fucked-up celebrity way of life. Celebrities all have ridiculous options. They have too much money, go to too many parties, and have way too many hot chicks who want to fuck them. So of course they all get divorced. But then everybody copies what TV and movie people do. Once normal people found out what celebrities were up to, they figured they could make power moves like that, too. It trickled down.

Normal people don't have the same opportunities as famous people, but they do have options. There are Internet dating sites designed specifically for hooking up divorced people—and even some for people who are still married. It's like the world is begging you to destroy your own marriage. And I think we're all very easily persuaded. Of course, after normal people get divorced, they might discover that divorced life isn't quite as awesome for them as it is for a celebrity. But hey—too late now.

I've already explained why I don't think relationships are for everyone. Remember all that stuff I said about why not every dude needs to have a girlfriend? It applies even more if you're thinking of turning your girlfriend into your wife. Getting divorced is a big deal, at least once kids or money becomes involved.

But just like with relationships, I don't believe that no one should ever get married. I've done it twice, and I would never say that I'll never do it again. You just need to know what you're getting yourself into.

For starters, there is absolutely no reason to rush into anything. I believe that you should be in a relationship for a minimum of five years before you get married. That's how long it takes to get to know someone. After a couple of years, you might feel like you're best friends with your chick, but hey—even best friends break up sometimes. You need to know that your bond with your chick is rock solid.

In my opinion, dudes shouldn't get married until their midthirties. And if the girl isn't at least thirty, she should be pretty close. I really don't understand why people are in a hurry to get married when they're super young. If you're in your early twenties, I don't even think you should be in a relationship. It isn't going to last. Believe me, there will be plenty of time when you're thirty-five to shackle yourself to another person for a few decades, if that's what you want.

Even if you think you've found your soul mate, if you're in your early twenties, why rush? Why change anything? If your girlfriend tells you that she needs to be married now, well, your girlfriend isn't that smart. Take a stand. If that annoys her and she wants to leave you because of it, then let her go. I just did you a favor. Anybody who needs to be married that bad is probably insecure. They're trying to fill a void, but they're going about it the wrong way. Marriage doesn't make you happy.

You also can't get married because you're afraid that your girlfriend is the best you're ever going to do. If you aren't as happy as you think you can be with your current girlfriend, then don't stay with her. You may think you're never going to meet anyone else, but that's bullshit. You're just letting your insecurities fuck you over. There are millions of chicks. Look around. They're everywhere.

Besides, you need to live a little before you settle down. Go to Thailand and do some things you maybe don't even tell people about when you get back. A lot of guys wait until they get bored with their marriage to do that. But then, when they come back, they have to live with the guilt. They have to look at their poor wives every day and think about all the creepy things their wives don't know their husbands did in Thailand. And it doesn't have to be that way.

You need to get some sexual experience under your belt before you settle down with a chick. From what I've seen, if the person you marry is the only person you ever have sex with, you will eventually live to regret it. There have to be a couple whores along the way. Not necessarily prostitutes, mind you. Just loose women.

You may think that racking up a certain number of sexual experiences might mean girls won't want to marry you. But in my experience that hasn't been the case. Eventually, in a relationship, the question is going to come up. How many people have you boned? For me, the answer is probably in the thousands. I've had sex with everybody. When I had that conversation with my first wife, back in

Australia, she thought I was insane. But then we were married for a long time. Sure, she beat me up all the time, but it wasn't because of all the people I slept with before her.

If you cheated on a lot of people in the past, that's a different story. We'll talk about cheating later on in this chapter. But if you got around when you were young but never promised anybody anything, and now you're in love and you want to marry your girlfriend, just be honest. If you just want to get someone in bed, then go ahead and lie your ass off. But if you've got a girlfriend and you want to keep her, tell her the truth. If somebody can't stay with you because you slept with twenty girls, then you probably don't want to be with her anyway.

And it goes both ways. I don't want my girlfriend to tell me she only slept with four dudes before me if that's not the truth. For one thing, it wouldn't be cool for her to lie to me. Plus, I'm looking for a girl who knows what she's doing in bed. In my world, you don't score any points by claiming you're a virgin.

I don't think a guy needs to stress out about how he proposes to his girlfriend. There's no wrong way to do it. You love your girlfriend, and you know what she likes. If she's going to say yes, she's going to say yes. And if she's going to say no, releasing a bunch of doves and balloons out of your ass isn't going to change her mind.

If you want to go for the big elaborate proposal, I'm sure your girlfriend will love it. She already loves you, and she knows what kind of guy you are. But even if you put no thought into it and just hand her the ring, if she loves you, she'll love that, too. Again, your girlfriend is already aware of what kind of guy she's signing up for. And besides, she probably already knows the proposal is coming. Girls usually figure that out. They always know what you're thinking—about everything.

I strongly recommend that you do not fuck anyone at your bachelor party. Don't tell me about how it's your last chance to enjoy the single life. Your last chance was before you got engaged. Would you go and fuck someone the night before you popped the question? Because that makes about as much sense. It's just as stupid as shooting a bunch of heroin in your eyeball, one last time, before you go to rehab.

And even worse, if you need to fuck a chick the night before you get married, then don't get married. You're going to cheat on your wife. It's not going to last.

When it comes to planning the wedding, I don't think a guy needs to be overly involved. It is her big day that you're planning, so you do need to at least look like you're interested in everything that's going on. You can't just stand around with your hands in your pockets. You need to pay attention to all the conversations. If you're not the kind of guy who's going to get really into wedding planning, your chick already knows that. But you at least need to do a respectable job of pretending to care.

Plenty of people stay in happy relationships for years and years without ever getting married. To me, the only reason you need to make it official is if you want to have a baby. And in that case, I really think you need to have some money in the bank. You're going to have to feed that baby and give it an education.

And after you get married and have kids, you can't just stay home and watch TV every night until the kid goes to college. That's probably not a recipe for a happy marriage. You need to have money for a babysitter, so you can take your wife out to dinner. From time to time, you need to able to go get a hotel room, and order champagne from room service, and fuck your wife while she's dressed up in a rabbit costume. I say "rabbit costume" metaphorically, of course.

Whatever your thing was before the kid came along, that thing can't just go away. And like it or not, babysitters, hotels, and rabbit costumes all require money.

It might be intimidating to think about committing yourself to several decades of sex with one person. But I don't think you can worry about that too much. I don't think waking up thinking about having sex with the same person for fifty years is a good way to start your morning. You have to take it day by day. I'm sure it'll work out if you're both still communicating.

It's not my favorite thing to imagine old married people having sex. But I have to think that if you're healthy and you take care of yourself, when you're sixty-five, you probably just keep banging away at your wife the same way you do now. People are really healthy these days. If you take your vitamins and drink your green drinks, then sixty-five ain't that old anymore. If you've got a bad heart, you're probably out of the game. But if you can get your heart rate up without worrying about dying, I think you probably just keep fucking.

There are probably positions you can't get into when you reach a certain age. The leg-around-the-head maneuver is likely going to fall by the wayside. Eventually, women's vaginas fall out, and dudes' penises don't go up. But if your shit is in working order, I say you slap it out like there's no tomorrow.

I think there will come a time where even I will get sick of sex. I used to want to skateboard all the time, and now I'm sick of that. At some point, I think I'll just want to go to the park and walk my dog. I'll just want to have a cup of tea and think about the days of old. I really don't see myself being seventy-five years old and still fucking new chicks and getting my girlfriend to film it. I think that's just a phase. I really do.

Being married is hard work. You've got to handle all your normal adult responsibilities, and you also need to keep the spark alive. You need to go to work every day and pay your bills. And then after you have kids, you need to come home after work and spend time with them. And then, after the kids go to sleep, you can't just crack a beer and sit on your ass. You need to get to work fucking your wife from multiple angles. You need to think of ways to stay romantic and keep her happy. You need to buy her flowers. It doesn't matter if flowers are lame. When it comes to relationships and marriage, being lame is cool. And being tough is stupid.

I may be divorced now, but there was a time there where I was a really good husband. And I can tell you that when I was handling all of my shit at a high level, I did get results. You have to be super romantic. Some chicks are more into that than others, but if a girl tells you she's not the romantic type at all, you need to know that she's lying.

You have to think about her, all the time. They know if you're constantly just thinking about football. Remember the way you treated her when she was your new girlfriend? Well, you can't just let that feeling die. You need to get creative. You need to think of different things you can do with her and do for her—and it can't just be things that involve your penis going inside her vagina.

I always liked hiding little notes. If you hide them somewhere good, it goes a long way. And you don't have to be a poet. "I love you" is great. You don't have to say anything more than that. You definitely don't need to get all gross and sexual. You don't want to write "My cock misses you"—unless you've got a "My cock misses you" kind of relationship.

Buying expensive gifts all the time is great, if you can afford it.

And you should send her flowers on random days, not just for Valentine's. But if a girl is only happy with gifts that cost a bunch of money, then I don't think that she's the chick you should have been going for in the first place. It really is the thought that counts. Make the effort to learn what she really likes. If she sees that you made an effort, a lot of times that's good enough. If you know how to make stuff, then make her something. If you don't know how to do anything, that's even better. Put some time in and make a massive painting. Express your love for her with your complete artistic incompetence. Chicks dig that.

You also need to make an effort to keep yourself in shape. Some people think after they get married they can just kick back and get fat. And that is a major mistake. When you got married, you signed a contract that says you are going to try to remain fuckable as long as humanly possible.

Of course, the same goes for her. Your wife also needs to keep making an effort. She also signed a contract that says she won't slack off and get lazy and let herself go. If your wife gets fat and it honestly doesn't bother you, then I guess you might want to skip the drama. But if my wife got fat and I wasn't happy about it, I would just tell her straight up. There are other ways to go about it. You could tell her that you wish you both ate healthier or suggest that you both go to the gym together. Just know that you're not fooling anybody. If you think she's fat, she's going to figure that out. Sooner or later she's going to catch you giving her a look. You're dealing with a person who is more advanced than you.

It's better to address the situation head-on. If my wife was getting tubby, I would call it before it got out of hand. When the situation is still fixable, it's not quite so hard for her to hear about it. But if you wait until she's 250 pounds, you're probably fucked. She's probably not coming back from that.

If you're getting just as fat as she is, then you don't have a fat leg to stand on. You just have to shut up and deal with having a fat wife. But if you're fit and she's not and the situation is getting worse, then you need to handle that. You need to tell her that the kitchen is closed after seven P.M., just like you would with a child.

Once kids come along, of course everything changes. That's to be expected. I understand that chicks get weird about their bodies after babies come out of them. Something comes over them. It's like they can feel the goddess of motherhood watching over them at all times, so they get weird about putting their legs behind their head when they're boning their dude.

So the guy needs to do his part. If you're the husband, you need to make your wife feel loved and sexy. That has become one of your main jobs, even more so than before. She has so much shit she has to do with the kids every day. It's going be hard for her to flip into sexy mode. But believe it or not, there are women who can spend their day wiping shit off a baby's ass and then still look forward to getting your come on their faces. In some relationships, that really does happen. It's just that dudes get lazy. Everybody does.

I know that some women pull completely back from sex after they have kids, and no matter what the guy tries, there's nothing he can do about it. If you're in that situation, you have my sympathy, but I also feel like you can't be totally surprised. If that's the way your wife is now, you should have known that before you had a baby with her. Back in the beginning, she had to have given you some clues that that's the way she is. She probably wasn't into it from the start. If your wife doesn't really want to have sex anymore after she has kids, and you're okay with that, then I guess that's okay. But if that happens to me, then me and my wife are no longer sexually compatible, and that's a problem.

If, for whatever reason, you find that there's a big difference in your sex drive and your wife's sex drive, you need to do something about it. That alone could be the seed of destruction for your marriage. You need to go to a therapist to have that conversation, because otherwise there's going to be a fight.

The two of you can find a way to meet in the middle. That can be done. But if you and your chick can't do it, either you need to decide that sex is not that important to you, or you need to break up.

From guys who call in to the show, I've learned that sometimes, not only does the sex go away after babies, but the dudes also aren't allowed to masturbate. If you are a woman in that kind of situation, my question for you is: Why are you so mean? I'm not allowed to fuck you anymore, and now I can't touch my wiener, either? That is satanic.

If you're not going to fuck your husband, he deserves to be able to get massages with happy endings. And if you can't handle that, well, then you need to fuck off. You have forced your husband to decide between living a life with no sex and getting a divorce.

If your chick pulls an about-face on you after you get married but before you even have kids, then you need to be very concerned. The biggest mistake you can make is not realizing that after kids come along, it isn't going to get better. It's probably going to get worse. If you know the chick you were dating isn't the same chick you're now married to, you need to get out of there. She's going to get even crazier once you have kids. And then you're going to be involved with her for the rest of your life. You're never going to get rid of her.

If you don't have money or kids, then getting a divorce really isn't a big deal. Maybe it is to your grandmother or something, but that's about it. If you're young when you get married and then you have a good, clean divorce, it's the same thing as breaking up with a girlfriend. It just costs a bit more.

Of course, the big whopper that can ruin a lot of marriages is infidelity.

If you're in any kind of relationship and you want to cheat, then that tells me that you don't actually want to be in a relationship. If you just wanted to sleep with a bunch of people, then you shouldn't have even gotten into a relationship in the first place. You should have just had sex as much as possible, without committing to anybody. Like a broke-ass George Clooney.

If you're honest with yourself, then deep down, you know if you're going to cheat or not. It's not that hard to figure out. And if you know deep down that you could cheat, then you should not get married.

That's the smartest advice I can give anyone. I know it's the harder road, but it's the better road. Sure, you'll be lonely every now and then, but that's the price you have to pay. I see that now, because of the people I've hurt. I feel like I've taken people's innocence, in a way. I don't think that's a cool thing to go around doing. It took me forty fucking years to even understand how bad infidelity can truly be.

Nobody gets out alive. I have a daughter, and I know now that girls who are a part of unfaithful relationships have issues. I have a son, and I don't want to see him grow up and be like that. You can't just have everything. Even famous basketball players who get to have a wife and still fuck everybody on the side, I'm telling you, it's not what it's cracked up to be. That shit is dangerous. It's fucking expensive. And you can give permanent emotional scars to people that you love.

If you catch your wife cheating, chances are she wanted to be caught. Once again, they're smarter than us. It's very rare that a married woman will put herself in a situation where photos of her fucking some dude in a closet blackout drunk will accidentally show up on Twitter.

If you're a dude and you get caught red-handed, then don't fight it. If I get full-on Tiger Woods busted, then I just say I'm sorry, and then I'm gone.

Bottom line, if you're married and you don't have kids and you flagrantly catch the other person cheating, it's just over. I am a cheater, and I'm telling you once somebody cheats, that's it. I'm not saying you can't change, but it ain't going to happen any time soon. You don't cheat one day and then the next day make the resolution that you'll never do it again, and actually stick to that. People don't just cheat for no reason. There are issues at work that need to be resolved.

So just move on. You're done.

Unless there are kids involved. In that case, what you want to do is to drag it out and make it hurt as badly as possibly for as long as possible. And *then* break up. Strap yourself to the rack for a couple years, so you can tell yourself you tried.

Of course, cheating isn't the only reason a marriage can end.

If your wife kisses you funny, or she doesn't want to have sex with you anymore, that might be a sign that she's checking out. If she goes out with her friends all the time, even when you ask her not to, that's probably not good. If you're fucking her, and you open your eyes, and you see her looking out the window, the spark may officially be gone.

That happened to me. One time, years ago, I was having sex with my girlfriend. I wasn't actually married to her, but we had been on and off for like ten years, and I was sure I was going to marry her. At one point, I even bought a ring. Anyway, one time, I was boning her, lost in the moment. But then I opened my eyes and she was just staring out the window while I pumped away like an idiot.

I was too young and inexperienced to realize it at the time, but looking back, the moment that happened, me and her were done.

_9_

HOW TO BE A CHICK

SO FAR, THIS BOOK HAS focused on all of the moronic things that dudes do wrong. But as you might imagine, I have a couple of thoughts for all you ladies out there, too.

If you don't know that much about me, or if you've just caught my radio show here and there, you may assume that I think all women are stupid or evil. You might guess that I only see women as sex objects or something like that.

But that couldn't be farther from the truth. I truly believe that men are significantly stupider than women. I think girls are way more organized than we are and that they have a lot more common sense. On average, I also think women have more love in their hearts than men do. Women are way more considerate of other people and more able to feel other people's pain. I'm not sure why. Maybe testosterone gets in the way of dudes giving a shit. It's like it's a girly trait to care about other people. But compassion seems like it's part of the female nature, and I believe it's one of those things that make the world go round.

How was that? Do you believe me now?

Okay—one more time, let remind everyone that I love women, and I have zero respect for guys who disrespect females. And, ladies, please remember that everything I'm about to say is for your own good.

There are a bunch of things that women think they know about men. For example, most girls probably still think there's nothing dudes love more than a girl with huge tits showing off tons of cleavage. But you couldn't be more wrong.

Ladies, if you have big tits hanging out of your shirt, to us, that makes you look like a whore. You need to be careful about just how much cleavage you want to show off. When your boobs are bursting out, that tells guys that you don't mind if we stare at them. It also tells a guy's friends that if he hooks up with you, they have a right to make rude comments about you afterward. So if you've got big tits, keep them covered, unless you want everybody to think you're stupid. If you have massive boobs, most of us actually think it's cooler if you keep them a little bit hidden.

At the same time, if you have little titties, you might think there's no point in exposing any part of them. The idea that guys don't like little sporty boobs is ridiculous. No man can deny sporty boobs.

Personally, I like them better. Saying that all guys prefer huge boobs is like saying that all women dig ten-inch dicks. It's just not true.

A lot of girls think men only like chicks who are super skinny. But I'll take a girl with an ass over a supermodel any day. Personally, I like a girl who's a bit thicker or stockier, particularly if it's because she has some muscle. I'm more into chicks who are fit than girls who are just skinny. And if a fit girl can really do stuff with her body, that's especially impressive to me.

Lots of girls think that looks are the only thing that matters to men. Sure, we all love hot chicks. You know that. But looks can only get you so far. For example, everybody wanks on about that Kate Upton chick. But I look at her, and I just see a humongous cheese sandwich. I have never met Kate Upton, and I'm sure she's a very nice lady. But I don't see a bunch of very interesting things going on in her brain, behind the smile. She looks boring, and potentially very lame in bed.

Especially as I've gotten older, I've really come to appreciate girls who are good at stuff. I think that's gnarly to all dudes. Personally I've never gone out with a girl who's successful in her career and stuff like that, but that's probably just because I'm insecure. I've always thought that women like that are better than me. But I don't see too many successful women who don't end up with high-level dudes. Being legitimately good at stuff makes you a catch.

On the other hand, there's a bunch of stuff girls do that guys hate. And a lot of it is stuff you're probably not aware of.

Let's start with a biggie: Girls shouldn't say "dude." They shouldn't say "bro." If you're a white girl, just because you used to go out with a gangbanger, that doesn't give you the right to start all of your sentences with "homie" this and "homie" that.

And, even more than men, girls shouldn't show off how loud

they can burp. Along the line, maybe you hung out with some gross dude who burped all the time and didn't care when you did. But I can assure you that is not the case with most of us. And that goes double for farting.

If you can do pussy farts and you think that's funny, I disagree. And yes, this has happened to me. It was a long time ago, but I remember it like it was yesterday. A girl at a party said, "I can do fanny farts. Want to hear me do one?" ("Fanny" means "pussy" in Australia. Naturally, this happened in Australia.) Of course I did, and I laughed when I heard it. But in the back of my head, all I was thinking about was how nasty she was.

Spitting is actually not that annoying. If you have to do it, you have to do it. You can't just be swallowing loogies. But if you do it more than once in a night, then maybe we've got a problem.

To me, cigarette smoking is a whopper. You may think it makes you look edgy or sexy, but smoking is probably my number one turn-off. Cigarettes make you smell and taste like shit. And if you're a girl who's on the pill, it's scientifically proven that if you smoke past the age of thirty-five, there's like an 80 percent chance you're going to have a heart attack. So smoking shows me you're a fucking moron whose face stinks.

I went on a date about a year and a half ago with a girl who smoked. She tried to come over to my house after finishing a cigarette, and she was like, "I brought a toothbrush." As if that helps. Brushing your teeth right after you smoke just makes you taste like toothpaste and cigarettes. That stink doesn't go away that easy.

And, man or woman, littering with cigarettes is beyond bullshit. I do not understand why cigarette smokers who would usually never dream of littering with anything else can convince themselves that a cigarette butt is not trash. Not only is it made of paper, but there's poison in it. You just dropped a poison pill on the ground. And, at least where I live in California, that poison is going to go straight into the ocean, where it will kill the things you and I both live off of. If you're going to smoke, put your cigarettes out in your fucking ashtray, and then empty your ashtray into a garbage can. If you don't like the way it makes your car stink, then don't do it to planet Earth.

Even if you don't smoke, you need to make sure your breath doesn't smell. Bad breath doesn't work for anybody, but it's even worse on a girl. Girls need to be more on top of maintenance than guys do. It's just a fact. So if you can't even keep your mouth clean, then I just assume you have a garbage disposal for a vagina.

Girls really need to be aware of how they laugh. If you've got a really loud or annoying laugh, I would try to tone it down. If you snort when you laugh, that's actually kind of cute. But, speaking for myself, those witchy kinds of laughs get under my skin. If you are one of those girls who never stop laughing, maybe at first it will make me feel cool that you find me so hilarious. But if you're super over-the-top, eventually everyone around you will want to kill you.

If you ask a guy, he'll never tell you the truth. It takes a really good friend to say you have a stupid laugh. But if you think you might, then ask somebody. And if your laugh is indeed as stupid as you suspect, I would definitely not unleash that around a guy until you have already made babies with him.

Little things girls do when they're hanging out can be irritating. Don't look at your phone all the time or constantly finish sentences before I can get them out of my mouth. You also don't want to flick your hair all the time or make too many adjustments to your face. Those just tell me you're insecure, and, as I've said many times, confidence is the key.

Talking about ex-boyfriends can be bad. There's definitely no place for that on a first date. If we're seeing each other, and you've got kids, and your ex is in your life, you're going to have to bring that up sooner or later. But if you just have an ex-boyfriend that you don't like, don't bring it up until we're full-on boyfriend and girlfriend. That's when I want to know more about your life, both the good and the bad. That's the right time to hit me with the bad.

Sometimes, bringing up ex-boyfriends is an attempt to start up mind games. And I don't go for any of that shit. I'm so well trained at this point, I don't even take the bait anymore. If a girl starts telling me about some other guy who was telling her how hot she is, I zone out after half a sentence. I literally don't even hear it.

Speaking of being fucked up in the head, we've probably all known women who are attracted to bad boys. And when I say "bad boy," I really mean "asshole." Just because a dude has a bunch of tattoos or rides a motorcycle, that doesn't make him a bad boy. A bad boy is a guy who keeps telling everyone to fuck off.

I don't think it really works out for girls when they try to date assholes. If a guy doesn't like society telling him what to do, then guess what—he isn't going to want you telling him what to do, either. This is the kind of guy who will fuck your friends when you pass out. When he gets drunk at bars, he will punch dudes in the face for looking at your ass. When you go out with that guy, you get what you deserve.

I haven't done much research into the subject, but I would guess that a lot of girls who date assholes also have dads who are assholes. If you're a nice girl and you keep ending up with assholes, then go to therapy. You've got issues.

When it comes to the way you look and the way you dress, there are things that tons of girls can pretty easily improve on. It's amazing that I should even have to point this out, but girls need to wear clothes that fit. If you're trying to wear something tight and you're not super shredded, you need to check and see if some fat is blubbering out the sides of your jeans. We all appreciate that you're trying to look sexy, but it doesn't make you look like dating material. Only drunk dudes are going to try to bang you.

If there's something wrong with your face that can be fixed, you need to get on that shit immediately. If your teeth are crooked, what are you waiting for? And if you've got a big bent nose, then get a nose job. I know that sounds harsh. And I know not everybody has the money. But if I'm a twenty-year-old chick, and I've got a hooked nose, I'm going to shave it down. If you do, life is going to be so much sweeter for you. I know it sucks. I know it's evil. But that's the way of the world. I'm bald now, and I've made my peace with it. But before I shaved my head, if there was a nose job equivalent I could have gotten to keep my hair, you bet your ass I would have done it.

I don't think there's anything wrong with a little bit of plastic surgery. It wouldn't bother me at all if a chick I was dating had fake tits, or a nose job, or ass implants. Who cares, as long as it looks good? But a little plastic surgery goes a long way. If I can tell you've had a ton of work done, then so can everybody else. When a girl goes overboard, her nose gets too skinny, her lips get too fat, and worst of all she looks exactly the same as a thousand other chicks who all invested in that exact same package. Girls who look like that probably think we're all staring at them because of how sexy they are. But really, it's because they kind of look like cartoons.

When it comes to makeup, less is more. I know every asshole says that, but it's true. You can overdo makeup, but I don't really think you can underdo it. A lot of times, chicks who are stupid hot can get away with some hot-pink 1980s bullshit. But if you're not that hot, don't attract that much attention to your face. Just keep it mellow. Besides, if you're really, really ugly, sometimes makeup doesn't even help. I hate to break it to you, ladies, but if you have really bad skin, makeup doesn't hide it. We can all still tell.

By the way, being ugly doesn't necessarily have to sink you. If you are a girl and you suspect that you're ugly, then for God's sake, do yourself a favor and get in shape. If your body's hot and you're a butterface, that still flies. Truthfully, super-fit people with ugly faces don't look that bad. That's why ugly gay dudes don't seem that ugly. If you're really fit, and you develop some style, and you get a cool haircut, then guys will probably convince themselves you just look "exotic."

Women don't think that guys notice their feet, but I am on those like a hawk, and I know I'm not alone. If your toes hang out the sides of your shoes, you'd be surprised how many dudes notice that. In general, if you don't have good-looking toes or if your little toes stick out farther than your big toes, then if I were you I wouldn't wear open-toe shoes too often. If the nail polish on your toes gets scratched, then you need to take it off, or else we can tell you're kind of dirty. If your shoes don't fit, or if you don't know how to walk in a certain pair of shoes, then don't wear them. Some dudes might not catch that, but most of us will. If you have cankles, I wouldn't recommend bringing too much attention to them. Maybe try boots.

Not sure what I mean by "cankles"? If you have cankles, that means that your calves go all the way down to your feet. You look like you don't have any ankles. It's not very attractive, but there are things you can do about it. I myself was born a cankle sufferer. I used to just walk around on my toes for years, until I changed the shape of my legs. It can be done. Hilary Duff used to have cankles, but she doesn't anymore. Sure, her head is now twice the size of her body. But, hey—no cankles.

When it comes to underwear for women, I think times are changing. I feel like G-strings are no longer that necessary. It used to look cool when girls had that string riding up their butt, but now it's over. G-strings and lacy stuff potentially send the message that you're a little bit old. They also send the message that you might be a stripper.

You probably want to replace any G-strings you're still holding on to with those little boy short panties. Those accentuate your ass, and having a butt is pretty important to most women these days. Blame it on hip-hop. Every woman has to have some kind of ass, and if she doesn't, she's arching her back to make it look like she does. It's just what you have to do to stay in the game. We are living in an ass world.

Speaking of asses, if a girl has a hairy butthole, I don't even get that. You are nasty. And if you've got a mustache, get it off. Wax it. Do whatever it takes. If it's not that fluffy, dye it. If you're a girl and you're not sure whether everyone can see your mustache and your unibrow, let me inform you that the answer is yes, they can.

Vagina hair is on the comeback trail these days. Trust me, I see a lot of vaginas. For a while, bald was the way to go, but now that's going out. So is the landing strip. Currently, a lot of girls are rocking the triangle. I think that works for everybody. No matter what your pussy style is, the main thing is keeping your look really tight. Women should maintain their vaginas like a black dude maintains his hair. Do that, and trust me, you'll never get a complaint.

Once you've gotten rid of your G-strings and you're paying as much attention to your pubic region as Jay Z does to his hair, you might want to send a man some sexy photos of yourself. Of course, most dudes would prefer that you send them pictures of yourself fully naked, spread-eagle, showing off your hole. That's just how dudes are. But you don't need to give in to that. If I was a girl, I'd just send photos of my shit covered. If you've had a boyfriend for years, and you love him, and you're trying to be hot, then you can send naked photos. It's still not safe, because you never truly know what will happen with your relationship or with those photos, but at some point there has to be some trust. I know when girls send me photos it goes a long way.

But here's the thing—on your iPhone camera, you actually don't look any better when you're fully naked. If you're really hot, you're going to look just as hot with panties and a bra on. And if you're not that hot, you're going to look even hotter in underwear. So in the beginning, your man gets no hole and no nipple. You've got so many reasons to keep it covered.

I think a lot of girls are unsure of themselves when it comes to handling penises. One of the biggest mistakes I see is chicks being too aggressive off the bat. When you first get ahold of it, there is no need for any rapid-fire jerking. Maybe you're a little nervous or a little excited, but I don't understand why you need to start jerking me off like there's no tomorrow in the first three seconds. You want to work your way up.

You also need to finesse the cock when it comes to blow jobs. Just like with hand jobs, it's not about just clamping on and going for broke. I can't give you a lot of technical advice for what to do when you put a penis in your mouth. But I can tell you what you should be thinking:

First things first, if you're not into sucking a cock, then don't even bother. I speak for all men when I say that we need to feel the passion. You need to fall in love with it. You need to worship it. You need to become one with the cock.

You need to play mind games with yourself. You need to tell

yourself that you're the best dick sucker that ever lived, and believe it, and then start acting like it. Tell yourself that you are the queen of sucking dick. After that, everything pretty much falls into place.

Beyond that, the most important thing is to make sure you don't injure my dick. If you've got any rings on, you should remember to take them off. These days, I feel like every girl has that twisty hand thing going during blow jobs. If you're doing that while you're blowing me and you've got rings on, then something might get pinched, and that ain't cool.

You've also got to watch your teeth. If your teeth hit my penis once, okay, whoops, whatever. But then you need to make an adjustment. Don't repeat the same move over and over, or it's going to happen again. I would say three teeth hits in the same spot and we're moving on to something else. Depending on how hard your teeth hit, we might be completely done.

It might surprise you when I say that a woman does not need to swallow. If you used to swallow, and then you get married and you stop, then I will see you in hell, because that's pretty fucked up. But if swallowing loads isn't your thing from the get-go, there's a way around it. If you don't want it in your mouth, you can talk to your guy about it and direct it somewhere else. If a dude is about to come and you grab his dick, tell him to shoot on your tits, and then direct it to your chest, I promise you he will still be a happy man.

In general, it's very hard for a man to deny a woman when she is commanding his come. If a guy is having trouble finishing, you can usually command the load out of him. If you're having sex, and you're ready to be finished but he's not, try that move. If it doesn't work, then feel free to give up. It wasn't gonna happen anyway.

A woman doesn't always have to swallow, but I do believe that girls need to be comfortable with loads. If a girl is grossed out by your come, then she's not ready to have full-on sex. Sex is messy. There are vaginas in your face, and you're licking holes that people pee out of. That's the deal. If a girl doesn't want to touch come, that tells me that either she's too young to be ready for adult sex, or she's never going to be ready for it.

A woman should also be comfortable saying sexy shit in bed. Women all know that men like it when you talk dirty in bed. But you might be unsure about exactly what you're supposed to say.

If you're shy and you just need a starter kit, I would recommend anything about your man's cock. "I love your cock." "I want to suck your big cock." Those ones are great. You can't go wrong complimenting a man's penis. If it's on the small side, maybe don't bring up how hot his huge cock is. He's not stupid. Just go with how much you love the dick.

Or just tell him you want him to fuck your pussy. Cock and pussy—those are bangers. They're forever. The classics.

For me personally, the creepier a girl talks in bed, the better. But there's no need to talk like you're in porn every time we're having sex. There's a time and a place for that. There will be times when you're drunk and for whatever reason the sex is getting a little more aggressive than usual. That's a good time to yell at my dick or whatever. But if that's your go-to move every time, then where can we go from there?

There's also a time and a place for rough sex. Despite how it might seem, my girlfriend and I do have sex softly sometimes. But lots of times it gets rough, and I know that she likes it. She likes that I'm strong and she likes that I can hurt her a little bit. I know she actually wants it harder than I'm willing to give it to her. And that's good with me. I'd rather underdo it a little bit. I'm really not what I look like.

The problem is when women who are into rough sex decide to inflict pain without any advance warning. You need to feel that one out a bit. Don't scrape your nails down the middle of my chest unless you have an inkling that I might enjoy that. Work your way up to that.

A long time ago, I was fucking a chick, and even though I never gave her any indication that I was into masochism, out of nowhere she bit me on the forehead. She did it so hard it actually hurt. I instinctively threw her out of the bed. She landed on the floor.

She was like, "Are you serious?"

As a matter of fact, yes I was. Dead serious.

There was a mark on my head. I made her leave. That was the first time and the only time I've ever kicked someone out of bed. Who does that?

A final thought on the subject of sex: As I believe I have established by now, I'm always on the lookout for a girl who doesn't think it's gay to lick my ass. Ladies, get with the times, and start putting your fingers up dudes' asses.

Once you're in a relationship with a man, the trick is to not let everything change from the way it was back when you were first dating. You still need to have sex as often as possible and say creepy shit while you're doing it. Loads to the face still make the world go round for him. Naked photos still go a long way, too. Grab his junk all the time. The important thing is keeping the spark alive.

Get creative. Ask your man to send you naked photos, too. Especially if he's hideous. A dude should always make a girl feel like a lady, but you need to always make him feel like a man, too. Compliment him on manly things. If he's working his ass off to help support the family, you should let him know it is appreciated, even if he shrugs it off. In general, if a guy shrugs off a compliment, that doesn't mean he's shrugging it off on the inside. It feels goofy for a dude to accept a compliment with a smile. But trust me—it went in there. Maybe some women don't know this, but shrugging off a compliment is just the manly way to say thank you.

When it's his birthday, take a minute and figure out what he's really into and what he really wants. Get him a new helmet for his motorcycle. Try to figure out what one of his really good dude friends might get him, and then do that. Or just make him one of those books with little coupons he can rip out to cash in for blow jobs and massages and shit like that. Those go a long way.

Just as a man expects certain things from his wife, a man also expects things from the mother of his children: She needs to help the kids be smart and well behaved. She needs to teach her kids common sense. She needs to give the kids rules, and then those rules need to be reinforced all the time. Those are a mom's main jobs. If the mom stays at home while the dad goes to work, he needs food on the table when he gets home. He needs all the shit in the house to be organized. And yes, she still needs to lick his ass.

In conclusion, here are some parting words that I believe all ladies can benefit from:

Start jogging now, so when you're older you don't turn into a bag of shit until it's absolutely unavoidable. You might be one of those twenty-year-old chicks who tells everyone you can eat like a fat dude and not gain weight. But believe me, someday you will. I always tell dudes that Father Time is coming for them. Well guess what, ladies—Father Time wants a piece of you, too.

Go to school and get an education. Otherwise you'll end up as a stripper. Or you'll end up working at Subway when you're forty. Which isn't much better.

16

HOW TO BE A FATHER

ONCE YOU RETIRE FROM THE getting-laid circuit and decide to get married, the next big milestone to think about is having kids. I have two, and they are the loves of my life.

As you can probably guess by now, I do not think every man should have children. In my opinion, there are plenty of people out there who definitely should not. If you and your wife are reasonably intelligent, that's a good start. If you have a good job and enough money to support a family and send your kids to school, then I would give you the green light.

But if you and your chick are both dumb, and you have no money and no job, then I don't think you should reproduce. If you are insane and your girlfriend's insane, too, then sorry, but I don't like your kid's chances. I am opposed to breeding more stupid insane people. I don't know why you would choose to do that. No one is going to win. Feel free to have sex with stupid crazy chicks if that's what you want to do. But for the love of Christ, wear a condom.

As everybody knows, you pay a steep price for bringing even normal, well-adjusted children into this world. It costs a lot of money. It's constant hard work. And you should be ready to not have sex. I don't care who you are—having kids is really hard on your sex life.

You don't sleep. When my daughter, Devin, was a baby, sometimes she would wake up in the middle of night, and she absolutely would not stop screaming unless you kept rocking her. I remember one night, at three A.M., I had to MacGyver a technique to keep her calm. I put her in her stroller and then tied a T-shirt to the handle. I would roll the stroller away from me, then reel it back in with the shirt. And I couldn't stop. If I so much as walked away to take a piss, she was hysterical again. But if I kept that up, she stayed quiet and at least I could watch some TV. I must have looked like I was sitting there bass fishing.

As a parent, many times you will find yourself living in a world of shit. Literally. And you can't just pass that off on your wife. I think it's complete bullshit if a guy thinks he doesn't have to change diapers because he's a man.

All in all, I think I got pretty lucky where shit is concerned. Unlike some of the stories you hear, I never had a baby shit in my mouth or anything like that. But I've had shit all over my hands, numerous times. And that is not my idea of a good time. You may think I do a lot of crazy stuff, but even in the most cracked-out periods of my life, I have never been into shit in any way. But when it comes to your kids, you just have to deal with it.

One time, Devin ate something that didn't agree with her, and then she shit her pants in the car. We pulled into the parking lot at a mall to change her. That's when we found out that diarrhea had rocketed all the way up her back. The car seat was covered in liquid shit. It was everywhere. I'm baby-wiping like a madman, and she's naked and crying. We had to run inside to get her new clothes.

While we were in the mall, we went to get something to eat. We're pushing her around in one of those strollers they'll lend you at the mall—the one that looks like a car, with the little steering wheel on it—and then Devin rocket-shitted all over again. There was rocket shit in the clothes I'd just bought her and rocket shit all over the stroller. It was on my shoes. Rocket shit got so many places that we didn't even find it all until later. It was that gnarly of an explosion. And then we had to go buy her even more new clothes. God knows how much money I spent that day, dealing with rocket shit.

And that's just what you deal with when your kid is a baby. And more importantly, that's just when you only have one kid. When you have two, it's a whole new ball game. People may tell you that if you have kids a certain number of years apart, then it's okay. But that's bullshit. When you have two kids, they fight each other all the time. I don't care what age they are. The fact of the matter is that they're two brainless drunk people who are constantly stuck next to each other, and they're sick of it. One of them always has to wait for the other one, for everything. Having two kids is twice as hard and twice as much work.

Your children will fight each other nonstop and test you constantly. And I'm just a baby in this game. The really crazy stuff is still to come for me. When your children grow up, they will do drugs and bring boyfriends around the house, and then one day they will have more babies of their own. Your kids can get sick. You think it's bad if something goes wrong with you and you need some kind of surgery? Imagine someone telling you it's your kid who needs that surgery.

It's torture. It's constant worry. For me, having kids means that I can never fully rest ever again. I don't think most people understand the magnitude of having a kid until long after they've had the baby. It takes having a child to understand how big of a deal it is to be a parent. It will freak your shit out.

But it will also be the best thing that ever happens to you. There are a lot of accomplishments I can point to in my life. But I can easily say that having kids is the coolest thing that I will ever do. No matter what happens, I know that I did something truly awesome, twice. To watch them grow up has been ridiculously amazing. I know how it feels to win skateboard contests and make thousands of dollars and then celebrate with a bottle of Cristal. I know what it's like to win a pro fight and to have famous people come on my radio show and tell me I'm awesome. And many times, just looking at my kids or hearing them talk has been right up there with any one of those other experiences.

That's why it breaks my heart when I see some people out there fucking up so royally as parents. I'm not perfect, but I've seen people do some amazingly negligent shit around their kids. I've seen people smoke cigarettes in front of their children at Disneyland. That blows my mind. Even if you don't flat-out murder your kids with second-hand smoke, you've got to be taking a couple days off their life span. And as a parent, that's pretty much the exact opposite of what you're supposed to do.

I see parents who let their kids throw crazy tantrums and do nothing to stop it. There's a way to handle that. You ask your kid what they're feeling. You listen to what they're going through. You try to help them sort it out. If you do all that and your child is still flipping out, then you take the kid to see somebody. Maybe a doctor tells you that your kid is spastic and they need to take some pills. But nine times out of ten, it's just happening because you're a bad parent. You need to pay attention to your kids. Plain and simple.

When Devin was first born, we took her to Australia. The flight was sixteen fucking hours. I did not sleep. And it wasn't because I didn't want to. This was back when I was still drinking and smoking weed, so I was pretty sedated on that plane. The reason I didn't sleep is because I couldn't just let my kid sit there screaming.

You get up, and you carry her around. You give her a bottle, or take her for a walk, or shake her a little bit. (I know that sounds bad, but there's a shake you can learn. It's actually more of a rocking motion. It takes a little practice, but there's a move a daddy can learn that can stop a kid from crying and still not give them brain damage. It's a happy medium.)

As I'm sure you've noticed if you've ever flown on a plane, some people will just let their kids sit there and go bananas. I guarantee you that same kid will grow up later and throw a tantrum and spin around on the floor like an asstard, all because you won't buy him a doughnut or something. And I'm telling you, it could have been prevented. If I was able to figure that out, there's no reason why everybody else can't.

I'm probably extra sensitive to that kind of stuff because of the way I was raised. My dad was a dick. Everything that I ever saw as a child was completely backward. I have learned what I know about parenting from experiencing the world and seeing what people with common sense do. Mainly, I copied my in-laws. They're a very serious, wholesome, all-American couple who raised their children to be kind and considerate. They're very good at raising people, so I just watched the fuck out of them and then applied all the lessons I was able to learn.

Look, if you wanted to get awesome at MMA, I bet you could find an instructor who wasn't a kook. And your kids are so much more important than that. If you look for some people who can show you what to do as a parent, I bet you can find them.

The most important part is just making time for your kids. I work a lot. I have a lot of shit to do, all the time. And it's important to get your job done or else you can't provide the things your family needs. But there's a fine line. If I work my ass off all the time, someday I might be able to buy five cars. But if that means I don't spend enough time with my kids, then I know I'll live to regret it. I can already see that.

And it's not enough to just be in the room. You can't be sitting there answering e-mails on your phone or worrying about what you've got to do that day. Work is stressful. Life is stressful. But you need to give your kids your full attention. You need to suck it up. If you're stressed or bummed out all the time, and you can't get past it, then you need to go see a therapist. Your traits will rub off on your kids.

And you need to be affectionate with your children. If you're a dude and you think there's something wrong with kissing your kids, then there's something wrong with you. If you're a man and you kiss your boy, that just shows that you love your kid. I kiss both my kids on the lips when they go to sleep. (Two or three kisses on the lips in a row? Okay, that might be a little odd.) I kiss them all over their faces. There will obviously be an age where you don't do all that stuff anymore, but even then you can still give them a kiss on the cheek.

On a day-to-day basis, your kids don't want much from you. They just want to play. Make eye contact with them. Get on their level. When my son, Tiger, plays video games, I sit there with him and pretend I'm the announcer. And now he only wants to play that game if I'm announcing it. I made it more fun for him than when he's just playing by himself. Sure, I am very hilarious as a video game commentator. But really, he just wants me to watch him.

You need to listen to their stories. It's weird how some people get uncomfortable talking to a child. I talk to my daughter about princesses and all that shit. I listen to all the behind-the-scenes drama going on with her school plays. I pay attention to the songs they like. I try to sing along. If I don't know the words, I ask them to teach me. To look at me, you probably would not guess that I know all the words to songs from *The Little Mermaid,* but I do. And not just the famous ones. We had all the direct-to-DVD sequels, too. I know *The Little Mermaid*'s deep tracks. If your kids tell you what's going on in their life and you just tell them "That's cool" or "That's nice," you're not really paying attention. And they know it.

I make the time to just follow my kids around. We spend time looking at stupid shit in the backyard. You take them outside and throw balls at them, or wrestle with them, or throw them on the ground. They love that stuff. And all the time, you're talking to them.

And then, of course, I'm a very creative person. I can apply my creative energy and come up with things that make my kids especially excited to hang out with their father. When I had a house with a pool, I used to make waterslides for the kids out of MMA training mats. The mats would be half on the ground and half in the pool, and I would cover them with laundry detergent so they were really slippery.

I have Speedos on when I go in the pool, and I have to wear a cap or else my head gets burned. When I have that stuff on, I am known to my daughter as Captain Underpants.

Captain Underpants has a bunch of toys that he puts on the edge of the waterslide, and then he hides underwater. When the kids try to steal Captain Underpants's stuff, he comes up to the surface and pulls them under. Then one of the kids has to come in and save the other one. Then usually that one gets caught while the first one gets away. A good parent is not afraid to look like an asshole. If you don't look like a dumb motherfucker from time to time, you're not doing it right.

Bottom line: To your kids, you are a superhero. If you're a dude, remember how you felt about Spider-Man when you were ten years old? That's how your kids look at you. You're Spider-Man. And if Spider-Man had some important life lessons to share with you, you would have listened. Stay in school. Eat your vegetables. Spider-Man gets to be preachy as fuck.

At the same time, there's no sense in trying to convince your kids you're perfect. Eventually they're gonna figure out you're not. And in the meantime, that might make them think that they have to be perfect, too. One time, I told Tiger that I don't feel any pain. I could see in his face that he truly believed me. He was blown away. I had to correct myself right there. I explained to him that Daddy has broken a lot of bones, and that after a while you get a little bit used to it. But yes, I told him, Daddy does feel pain, all the time. I felt like if I didn't say that, he might start to develop a complex. He might think he's a huge vagina because he's not impervious to pain.

You do have to be careful how you talk to kids, because you never know how they'll react to different stuff. Recently, I saw on the Internet that a guy who rode freestyle moto had gotten injured and died. When I saw it, I just reacted out loud. I said, "Oh my God!" And then of course the kids wanted to know what was up. I explained to them that Daddy's friend—a friend of a friend, really—had passed away riding moto. I told them that it freaked me out a little bit, because that sport is so dangerous.

Tiger immediately told me that he wants to ride freestyle moto when he grows up. "No way, dude," I told him. "There is no way you're going to do that."

And then he started crying. I didn't even realize it for a second. Then I asked him what was wrong. And Devin was like, "He's crying because you said that he's not allowed to be in freestyle moto."

Now, of course, I found this hilarious. But one of your jobs as a parent is not laughing at your kids when they are crying. I had to talk to him.

That was the first time I ever told him that he's not allowed to do something with his life. Look, I do not want my kids getting hurt for a living. Too many of the jobs I've had have involved me getting seriously injured. And if I have anything to say about it, my children will not walk down that same path. Tiger is not going to be a moto dude. He's not going to be a fighter. He's not going to be a skateboarder. Whatever else he wants to be, I will support him 100 percent. But if he wants to be in freestyle moto, I will use all my connections to fuck his career so hard. I'm not even lying. Maybe you don't agree with me, and maybe it's never the right move to interfere with your kid's dreams. But that's where I draw the line.

The same goes for Devin. If Devin ever wants to make a decision that will ruin her life, I'll lock her up. She is mine. I made her. If she wants to run away to Paris and become a pop singer, I will subject her to Muay Thai leg kicks. She will sit in her room until she figures out how to grow up. For her own good.

At the moment that Tiger was sitting there crying, though, I had to calm him down. I just told him that he could ride freestyle moto when he turns eighteen. That's a long way away, and he'll forget. Lying a little bit here and there is also part of being a parent.

At this point in my kids' lives, I really don't think there's a difference between raising boys and raising girls. Later on that will change. But I don't see any reason to instill boy values in Tiger or girl values in Devin. I don't see them as a boy or a girl, yet. Devin can be emotional about stuff, but so can Tiger. I think you should just treat kids based on their personalities. Some dudes' personalities are very girly, and some girls' personalities are very boyish. You have to treat them accordingly. If a girl doesn't want to play with dolls, then you don't need to force it on her.

When it comes to my kids, Devin doesn't always want to express her emotions. She's very emotional, but sometimes it's hard to get her to tell you why. Sometimes I believe that, just like myself, she doesn't even know the reason why. So you need to really communicate with her to find out what the problem is. It can be hard. Tiger is a lot easier. He's a bit of a crybaby. He'll tell you exactly what's bothering him, assuming you can understand him through the blubbering.

When Tiger gets a little bit older, there will be things that I need to instill in him. There are certain lessons every man needs to teach his son: How to be a gentleman. How to handle drama. How to handle fights. Shit like that. The things you do and do not do to women. I will teach him chivalry. I think the more a man teaches a young man to be respectful to women, the better the world is.

It's funny—if you don't teach a dude how to act, he'll manage to figure out all the shitty things a guy can do all by himself. But without some help, he'll never figure out chivalry. Because being good is hard work, and you're not going to do it when you're a kid. You need to be pushed. And it's not Mom's job to teach those kinds of lessons. That's Dad's job.

I do have a little bit of a double standard when it comes to saying cuss words. I know both of my kids are someday going to say "fuck" around their friends. Every kid does. But if I catch Devin doing it, that will be a bigger deal than when I catch Tiger. I'm going to be a little harder on her. I don't think it's a good look for girls to cuss all the time.

I don't think Tiger should ever really go around my house saying "fuck." That's our home. That's not how you act around your family. But there's a time and a place. As a dude, when he's older and he's hanging out with his friends and drinking a beer, then he can say "fuck" all he wants. I will never say "fuck" to my daughter, and I will never be cool with her saying it to me. But when Tiger is eighteen or so, to me he'll be a man. And when you're a man, I talk to you like I talk to my man friends. Fuck yeah, homie.

But in the near future, nobody gets to say "fuck." I don't cuss around my kids. I don't want to get a phone call from school about what my kid said in class today. I know what I look like and how I come across to people. I know what I do for a living and what I do in my life. I don't need any extra heat.

Someday, there will come a time when my kids find out about my past. And I don't intend to hide anything. I will be an open book. Did Daddy do heroin with prostitutes? Yes. What do you want to know about it? In the scheme of things, my kids lead a very privileged life. But I'll explain to them that things weren't always the way they are now. Their daddy had a really bad upbringing. And when Daddy did heroin with prostitutes, he was in a really bad place in his life. He almost died a bunch of times, and it all went back to how bad his upbringing was.

But if you are my kid, you are not having that kind of childhood. You have no reason to feel sorry for yourself. When Daddy was little and he had a problem, he didn't always have someone to talk to. But when you have a problem, we have therapists working around the clock for you. You are loved and taken care of.

If my kids want to know what I think about marijuana, I'll tell them that I think it's pretty cool. But I'll also tell them that if you're young and you smoke it all the time and you don't get off the couch, then life is going to pass you by. When I started skateboarding, all the other kids had friends from school and went to parties all the time. But I didn't have any friends. I didn't go to school. I just went to the ramp every day.

I was a straight-edge guy for seven years. I paid my dues until I had some talent under my belt. And eventually, I went from being a guy who didn't go to parties to a guy who didn't have to wait in line to get into the club. To this day, I am still seeing the rewards of all the time and hard work I put into skating back when I was a teenager.

And I'll tell my kids that, too.

Getting divorced changes certain things about being a dad. I think I always knew that sooner or later I was going to split up with my ex-wife. A million times, I said a sentence to her that started with the words "When we get divorced." She would always say, "Why do you keep saying that?"

(Yes, I know—I'm a catch.)

I tried. Believe me. But I always knew what kind of guy I was.

I couldn't see a scenario where we were eighty years old and still together. Sooner or later, either I was going to walk off, or she was going to leave me. I am fucking impossible. One way or another, I was going to break her.

I didn't get divorced because of the kids. The only thing I didn't like was living with somebody else. But I miss being around my kids all the time. I miss being there at night and helping them go to sleep. I miss waking up with them every morning.

After you get a divorce, the number one rule is that you still have to be super cool with your ex. You have to communicate with each other, and you still have to hang out as a family. If there's a gap between how the mommy is raising the kids and how the daddy is raising the kids, the kids will learn to exploit that. That's where they can start to learn to lie. That's where they can start to learn to cheat. I mean, they're going to learn those things anyway. But you can't do anything to make it worse. When it comes to divorce, if a kid has an issue and the parents aren't communicating, the child can start to get a little fucked up. And on your own, either one of you might not pick up on it as quickly. That's why you still have to work as a team.

You need to be friends with your ex, no matter what. I know in some situations that sounds insane, especially if she fucked some other dude or something like that. But you just have to do it. You can't say bad things about your ex in front of the kids. That's what you signed up for when you had children. If you are a divorced dad, and you don't have a brain, and you're leaning on this book to help you sort some things out, let that be the one thing you remember.

You need to be nice to her. If she says, "Fuck you, motherfucker, you're not going to see the kids," you still need to be nice. Because "Fuck you, motherfucker, yes, I am!" isn't going to help. There's never, ever going to be the right time to blow up. If you lose control of your emotions, all you're going to do is fuck yourself. It's just like with road rage. If somebody cuts you off and hits your car, you need to just pull over and wait for the cops. Even if that guy starts calling you a fucking pussy, if you punch him, he wins. This is the same thing.

If your ex goes ballistic, you just need to kill her with kindness. If she suggests that you go fuck yourself, you say, "That sounds great. I just want to help!" Be passive-aggressive as fuck. Even if she calls you out on it. Tell her she's great. Lie to her face. One way or another, you need to keep the lines of communication open.

Divorce will break a weak man. I don't think it's much easier on a woman, either. But if you're not careful, the people you could end up fucking up the most are the kids.

Another way people fuck up their kids is by dressing them like idiots. I don't know how it used to be, but I feel like it's pretty easy to get decent kids' clothes these days. And yet you still see a lot of sad little toddlers going around looking very old-fashioned. You wouldn't wear a bonnet or a bow tie, so why should your kid? And if you actually would wear a bow tie, why does your son need to be as big of a loser as his dad? Just get him the kids' clothes of today. They sell them at Target. It's not that hard.

I would also be careful about letting your children Rollerblade. My children will never so much as touch Rollerblades, because I am a pro skateboarder, and that's just the deal. But, contrary to how it might come across on my radio show sometimes, I actually don't think it's so bad for normal little kids to strap on some 'blades. If that's what they really want to do, then I say go for it. Rollerblading is like wearing Skechers. It's pretty harmless when kids are little. But if they're still really into it when they're nine or ten, you better check yourself. You're leading them down a dicey path.

It's not easy to imagine what my life would be like if I didn't have kids. Watching them accomplish things like learning to ride a bike brings you back to your own childhood. It blows my mind to see my daughter do creative stuff. She can sing and make jokes. Sometimes, at night, when I turn the light off in her room, she holds a lamp under her chin and tells me campfire jokes. Or she tries to tell me scary stories. She knows they aren't scary. She just likes fucking with me. It's crazy to see her start to develop her own little sense of humor. It's amazing to see their brains really start to work.

Hopefully, having kids makes you responsible. For me, having kids meant it couldn't just be all about having fun and getting pussy anymore. The most important thing now is doing everything I can to take care of them to the absolute best of my abilities.

Now, because of them, it's all about taking over the world.

CONCLUSION:
HOW TO BE AWESOME

THROUGHOUT THIS BOOK, I'VE ATTEMPTED to pass along some helpful stories and tips. If you've listened to everything I have to say, you now know how to look cool, and act cool, and get laid. You know how to treat women and how to treat your kids. You also now know what to expect if you ever accidentally wander into a swinger party. I truly hope that I've been able to help, or at least give you a few things to think about. If I've accomplished that, then to me this book is a success.

But that's not where this story ends. This chapter is where you decide what you really, truly want to get out of life. And this is where I show you how to get it.

This is the final piece of the puzzle on the road to becoming awesome.

Having a cool job or cool stuff doesn't make you awesome. I don't think I'm awesome because I look cool and chicks want to fuck me. My belief in myself comes from the things I've been able to accomplish with my life, starting with my career as a skateboarder. All I ever wanted was to be a pro skater. And I did it. To this day, that still makes me happy. It never gets old. And my experiences on a skateboard directly led to all the other accomplishments that I've also been able to enjoy.

I'm awesome because of the mental attitudes I developed along the way to getting good at skating. I'm awesome because I face a lot of stuff that I'm scared of. I'm a very scared person, in many ways, and most of the time I don't act like it.

I'm awesome because all the skills I have are ones that I developed. And everything is worth more when you have to earn it. I think the closest thing to natural talent that I have would be my skill as a radio host. But I think even the talent I have for radio came from the life I had growing up. I'm good at moving a conversation around and getting people to like me. I think that was a necessary skill for me to have around my house when I was little.

People in my house were really aggressive. They were always quick to snap. So I learned that it was good to be cute and funny. I was always trying to keep people happy. At first it was my family members. Then I wanted all of my father's friends to like me. I don't think people always paid a lot of attention to me, but my dad's friends were always around. There was always a party going on, and I would try to entertain everybody. If I could make everybody laugh, then I could stay around. Otherwise, I wasn't allowed to be part of it. So in a roundabout way, I think I even put time into learning how to be great on the radio, all the way back then.

Like I've said before, I wasn't born awesome in any way. I made myself awesome. And if I can do it, then so can you.

Let's face it: Most people suck. When I'm in an optimistic mood, I don't always see it that way. But most of the time? Yes, that's what I believe. I don't even know how to say it without being a cocksucker. I believe most people lead average lives. They make average attempts to do average things. And I don't understand why.

I don't understand why you wouldn't test yourself, even just one time. Why wouldn't you try something crazy?

I believe that I will be a famous entertainer. One of the reasons I believe I will be famous is because when I talk to famous people I know, I see myself in them. I think a lot of famous people have something to prove, just like I do. Whether they are athletes or entertainers, they have a competitive nature.

We have an electronic punch pad on the radio show that measures how hard you can hit. We keep a list of everyone's scores, all-time, on the wall of the studio. And I notice that famous people always try to punch as hard as they can. And they always want an extra shot. All so they can have the best possible score on the fucking wall of a radio show. It's like famous people care more about doing well at everything they try (which of course can be a good and a bad thing).

I understand that not everybody is insanely driven to win everything all the time, like I am. But if you don't have at least a little bit of that drive, then I don't like your chances of becoming truly awesome. And that's sad to me, because you don't know what you're missing.

Remember the last chapter, when I said that looking at my kids was just as rewarding as winning any skate tournament?

I lied.

Having kids is great. It changes your life in ways you could never imagine. But with all due respect to my children, nothing is ever going to beat the feeling of winning skateboard contests back when that meant the world to me. I won a best-trick contest in England and got wasted for three months straight. I think I won $700, and I spent it all that night. And that was the fucking highlight of my life.

Everyone can be awesome if they want it bad enough. And I don't believe that anyone wants to be average. I think everybody desires greatness, at least at some point in their life. Everybody wants to go a little higher on the ladder of success. But I feel like the world beats most people into submission. You can get so down on yourself that the desire goes away.

Some awesome people were born insanely talented. But most of the awesome people I know are just normal people who were insanely driven. Anybody can be great. I'm not saying everybody has to become a professional action-sports athlete. If you're a young kid, but you're athletically fucktarded, why not start a band? Get a cheap video camera and go make a movie. If you're older, and you're in school, why not study harder than everybody else at your school, so you can get a really great job? If you already have a job, why not focus on your work like crazy and try to make way more money? If you hate your job, why don't you try to figure out something else you can do and then give that all you've got? What do you really have to lose?

If you feel like you've got nothing going for you and nothing going on in your life, then, believe it or not, this is the perfect time to start. That means you have time to figure out what your true passion is.

To me, without having something you're passionate about, there is no point in living. It's weird to me when people don't have a thing they really want to do. Especially young people. Years ago, I used to have an intern on the radio show named Wartcock. (I called him that because he had genital warts.) Wartcock was twenty-two years old. I used to ask him, over and over, what his dream was. What his mission was. And he didn't have an answer. That made no sense to me.

That's one problem I've never had. I've always known what I want to do. My problem is that I don't have enough time to be all the things that I want to be. When I was young, it took so much energy to stop myself from constantly adding more missions to my life. Sometimes I'd get on a tangent in my head. I'd hear an awesome song, and I would instantly say, "Fuck, I've gotta be a musician! I've got to get guitar lessons! And singing lessons!" And then I'd have to tell myself to calm down.

If you can't figure out what your passion is, then you're fucked. I can't help you. If you don't have passion for something, then you're going to quit. Because if you want to get really good at something, you're going to need to work on it all day, every day. You better try to find something you're passionate about fast, because the sooner you know what it is, the sooner you can move on to figuring out how to do that one thing exceptionally well. And that is going to take a shitload of time.

Obviously, my first passion was skateboarding. When I was a kid, I skateboarded all day every day. I got really good at it, and that's what gave me the confidence to believe I could accomplish other things with my life.

I am not exaggerating when I say that skateboarding made me awesome. When I first started skating, I used to hang out with these two twin brothers. One of them was really fat. The other one was straight-up obese. Neither of them could really skate, and yet at the start, both of them were better than me. But I fell in love with skateboarding, even more than they did. I went to the ramp every day. I couldn't stop thinking about it. Being great at skating was all I wanted. I wasn't spreading my effort around on a bunch of different stuff. I did one thing and one thing only.

I didn't have insane athletic talent. I don't have crazy leaping ability or anything like that. And I didn't come up with any brilliant tactical maneuvers to further my technique on a skateboard. I just outworked everybody. I saw kids come to the ramp and get good really fast. And I saw guys who sucked balls at the start. And then ten years later, I saw the guy with no talent kicking the shit out of the other guy, because he had it harder at the beginning, and that made him work.

If you put enough hours and dedication in, there will come a time when even your unathletic body and your stupid brain will start to put it all together. For me, it literally happened on one single day. All of a sudden I could do all these tricks, in my own certain way. And it was just because I went to that ramp every day, all day.

Years later, when I was a pro, somebody told me the theory that to get really great at something, you need to dedicate ten thousand hours to it. And that made sense to me. That's what I did when I was a kid, without even realizing it. Based on personal experience, I can tell you for a fact that if you wholeheartedly dedicate ten years of your life to your passion, then you will become one of the best people in the world at what you do. Most people don't make an effort to put ten years of their life into anything—although most of them accidentally put way more than that into a job that they don't even like. Think about that.

When I was a kid, I made half-pipes out of my mashed potatoes. And I don't mean one time. My parents always made me eat mashed potatoes for dinner, and every fucking night I skated the mashed potatoes, inside my head. I went to sleep thinking about it, and I woke up thinking about it. I made papier-mâché ramps in art class.

I got good at visualization. When I was learning tricks, I ran them through my head. I could see myself doing the trick. I could see myself looking at where I was going to land. And I could see myself riding away. I could see myself do a minute-and-forty-five-second ride. One hundred million times a day I would do that. Weeks before the contest, I was practicing my ride in my head.

I've always been able to do that. I think that's just from being a dreamer. As a kid, when I used to skip school, I would sit in an alleyway for I don't know how many hours. From whenever school started until whenever it ended. I was just running scenarios of glory through my head. And I don't remember being bored. I don't even have to close my eyes. I can just see things in my head.

You need to believe in your passion, no matter how stupid or insane that might make you look to the rest of the world. Did I think I could be a pro skater when I was sixteen? Fuck yes. There was never a doubt in my mind. Ever. Not even after the third time I paid for my own ticket to America and came back empty-handed. I just kept going back to the ramp. When I got off the plane from America, I would tell my dad to drop me off at the ramp, straightaway, and I would show everybody my new tricks.

It was an obsession. In the beginning, I didn't even have the athleticism of a fat child. And then I became one of the top three in the world. I probably could have won contests if I had stayed more dedicated when it really mattered. But if you ask people who know, there was a point—and maybe it was only one day—where I was the best skateboarder in the world.

When I went back to Australia years later with my daughter and I had a night out, I went down to the ramp and drank there. I just sat there and looked at it.

To me, that's where I built my empire. It might be a piece-of-shit empire compared to some other people's, but that's where I built me. That's where I built my confidence. That's where I made myself an athlete. On that ramp. Like Conan the Barbarian pushing that wheel around.

Once you find your passion, you have to think about it all the time. You dream about it at night. And when you're awake, you daydream about it. You fantasize about it. You do it every day, over and over again. You practice and you practice and you practice. That's where the passion is vital. If you're just lying to yourself about wanting to be great at something, then eventually you're going to give up. No man can just hold up a weight for the rest of his life. Eventually he's going to drop it. You've got to love it. It's the only way.

Once you have your goal, and you have the passion to achieve it, you need discipline. Every day that you're not moving forward, you're sliding a little backward. You're disrespecting all the work that you already put in. You have the power to control your attitude and the power to motivate yourself. You have the power to dedicate ten thousand hours to whatever you want. You don't need any help. Inside of yourself, you have everything you need to become awesome.

I used to write down a list of everybody who was above me in skateboarding. You can do it in your head, but for some reason, if you write it down, it seems to stick better in your mind. If somebody is better than you, then they know something that you don't. You need to figure out what that is. Obviously, you may need to come up with your own version of whatever they've got. But you watch people who are better than you and see how it's done.

That's what I did. And then I would pick people off. I would catch them, one by one, and work my way up the chart. You keep going until you're on top of it. I recommend starting with the weakest of the weak first, because beating somebody—anybody—fuels your confidence. It feels good to know you're moving up. If I'm going to try to break the world push-up record, then I don't think it would be a good idea to go for the record on my first day of trying. I would work my way into it. I would do what I could today and then try to beat that tomorrow. You're building confidence and taking people off the list.

When a goal is going to take years to achieve, it may be hard to stay focused. At times, you might not feel like you're getting where you want to be as fast as you think you should. You might think about giving up. That's why you need to keep your body and your mind sharp. You eat right, you sleep, and you drink water. When your mind is sharp, it doesn't quit as easily. I was lucky in that respect. When I was a kid, some older skaters got in my head and taught me that taking drugs and smoking cigarettes are for fucking idiots. I wanted to be down with these guys so bad, so I listened to them. Until later, at least. When you're trying to be the best, staying sharp will put you ahead of a lot of your competition.

Marijuana is something a lot of guys need to be careful with. Especially young dudes. I can't get totally down on weed. There was a time when me and my friends smoked weed every day. And at the same time, we were all getting really good at skateboarding, and we were all making money. But do I think I would have had more longevity if I didn't touch any drugs? Fuck yeah I do.

Some comedians I've met smoke weed and then it makes them really funny. If you're a surfer or a snowboarder and marijuana isn't stopping you from getting better every day, and you get a job out of it, then okay. I can see that. But if you're a kid, and you smoke weed all the time, and it makes you fucking sit there and eat potato chips, well, maybe now's not the time. For a lot of people, smoking weed is a part of growing up. But I don't think overdoing it when you're a kid works out for most people. I think the world is getting a lot higher than most people think. It's like a constantly sedated world that we live in. People have their beer, or their weed, or their pills. When you start to get to the bottom of it, it seems like everybody's got something.

Some of those people might even be your friends. Once you decide to be awesome, there are bound to be people who'll tell you it's impossible. Maybe it's a loser girlfriend or some loser friends. They're not going anywhere, and they don't think it's possible for you to make something of yourself, either. Or they're afraid you can, and that threatens their loser way of life.

Misery loves company. And you can only go so far with Team Loser. I truly believe that. I'm not telling you to get rid of your friends. But I can tell you that the better I got at skating, the higher the level of humans I got to meet. And they rubbed off on me and made me a higher-level human being.

If you're trying to get good at something, you are bound to have to deal with some failure. The only unfortunate thing about failure is that if you do it too much, you might get used to it. I think that not accepting failure is a key to success. Some people might tell you that you shouldn't take it too hard when you don't win. I say that's dead wrong.

I think the opposite is true. I think the pain of loss in a champion is much greater than the pain of loss in somebody who doesn't have the will to be the best. There were many contests where I emotionally broke down because I fell off my board. Looking back, even I would say I overreacted a little bit. Nobody died or anything. All it probably meant was I made like $600 less at that contest. But it was such a big deal to me.

The flip side of that is that when I put that much pressure on myself and I actually came through, winning was that much more glorious. I don't think the average person gets that hyped up for anything. Dealing with high-pressure emotions makes you feel alive. It's a cool thing to go through. It's a rush that can't be matched. It's almost like a near-death experience.

I think there are some people who do all the work and get really good at stuff, but then they choke under pressure. I've seen it. It's a very big deal. It can end careers. You get to the big show, but then you can't handle it. You're in front of a big crowd, and you can't get the people out of your head. You can feel all those eyes are staring at you, and it can fuck you up. I was never that guy, so I never had to worry about it. I think the more you like a crowd, the more the crowd tends to disappear, and I love nothing more than performing for a crowd. But I had a friend who came over from Australia with me who was totally like that. He had all the skills that I had, but he just couldn't hang.

Letting the pressure get to you comes down to your attitude, and once again, your attitude is your decision. Maybe there are some crazy deep issues that you need a therapist to work through for you. But I think most people just need to harden the fuck up.

The way I looked at it, I had skated so hard and broken so many bones. I had made it to America. Now all of a sudden I'm going to decide that I don't actually want to be there? Obviously people who get to that level do want it—a lot—but something gets weird when they get there. You need to figure it out. Otherwise, you will regret it for a long time to come.

If you put in the time and effort to get truly awesome at one thing, you will benefit from that experience for the rest of your life. You have the confidence that you can do the impossible, because you already got good at something. And when you've gone through the process once, you know how to become awesome at anything.

That's the secret: When you figure out how to be awesome at one thing, the same rules apply to the rest of the shit in your life. If you can figure out how to be awesome at playing cricket, then you can get good at getting chicks' phone numbers. You can get good at roasting fucking turkeys. School. Music. Anything. They all follow the exact same rules.

I didn't realize it at the time, but when I was out on that ramp, I was giving myself a blueprint for success. And not just for skateboarding. Now I know how to get good at anything.

The first step to being good at anything is to be obsessed with it. You need to be all in. You need to believe in yourself completely, even if no one else can see where you're going but you. No one but me believed that I could be a great skater. And in the beginning, no one but me believed that I could be awesome on the radio. If I really stood back and thought about the odds, maybe I would have been a little intimidated. But that's where ignorance works out for me. I'm a dreamer. I can make up my own world and believe in it so much and work for it so hard that I make it come true.

You need to also be obsessed with everyone who possesses any information you can use to make yourself better. When I was a kid, all professional skateboarders were gods to me. (A lot of them still are.) But when I got really into fighting, then all MMA fighters became gods. I pick people, and then I idolize them, and then I learn how to be them. That's how I do it.

You apply the tricks you learned getting good at your first passion to the next one. I used to use visualization for skating, and then I used it for fighting. I visualized punches. I visualized how to throw them and where I would stand. It's the only way. I see everything before it happens.

You surround yourself with people you want to be like and watch the things they do. When I was a skater, I copied other skaters. When I wanted to be a fighter, I copied things from my friend Mayhem Miller. I've always done that. I take pieces of everybody.

When I decided I wanted to commit myself to being a celebrity, I took a lot of tips from my friend Benji Madden. I started dressing differently. I am practicing to be in the limelight. I am in training to be famous. Celebrities have to have the total package. That obviously includes the way you look. And I feel like I look more like a celebrity from copying him.

Getting to know Benji also gave me confirmation that I was on the right track. Like I said, when you start to move up the ranks of anything, you have the opportunity to spend time around people who can help you. He was the first friend I had who had already made it in entertainment. When I first started hanging out with him and his brother Joel, they would ask me about my plans. They would give me little bits of advice. They would always tell me, "You've definitely got something here." And that fueled my dedication to the game.

Getting good at stuff becomes addictive. I wouldn't say it's always been the path to happiness, for me or for the people around me. Anything that I get good at becomes the burden of my life, because I'm on a never-ending quest to be better. And the better you get, the harder it is to beat the last thing you did.

But every time I've put the work in to get good at something, the rewards for me have been massive. I dropped out of school when I was a kid. I never really got an education. But because I got good at skating, I got into situations where brilliant people who had lots of money were sharing their time with me. And it rubs off. I listened to Ken Block—the man who started DC Shoes—talk every day for a couple of years. I've talked to Tony Hawk about all the things that he does. The average bear doesn't get that info.

Along the way to becoming the best, you will probably have to risk a lot. But you stand to gain way, way more. I am pretty successful, but I know some ludicrously successful people. And believe me, you do want to be like them. There are perks that come with being the best at something. If you want to go to a baseball game, nine times out of ten, you're not paying for tickets. And nine times out of ten, when you get there, you're not sitting where the normal people sit. If you go to a concert, say good-bye to the pit—you're going backstage, or your spoiled ass might not even show up.

And yes, if you become ludicrously famous, it will completely change the way girls look at you. Something happens to women when they speak to really successful dudes. You know the way we are when we talk to insanely hot chicks? When you can't even compose yourself? Money and fame turn the tables. That's the one time that really hot women act like we do. And that's a special thing. I guess it depends on who you are, but I think having a hot girl drool over you is a little bit of a childhood fantasy for every man. And that never happens. They always put up a front.

But let me put it this way: I knew Tony Hawk before he was really Tony Hawk. I remember when I was in a higher league than Tony Hawk. And since then, I've seen girls who were out of my league hit on Tony.

Money is also good. I'm divorced, so I don't have any. But again, I know people. The best thing about money is not worrying about money. Imagine not having to think about your bank account. Imagine being a responsible, sane adult and not even checking the balance before you decide to buy your wife a fucking Mercedes.

Of course, there's more to life than vaginas and shiny shit. That's not the only reason you should try to be as successful as possible. If you play your cards right, you might be able to do what you love instead of what you need to do to get by and provide for your family. I always wanted to be a skateboarder. And even if most of the world at that time didn't think that was glamorous, I did. So when I became a pro, I walked through my day with my head high.

I worked in a supermarket at one time, and I did not walk with my head high. When I worked at an electronics store, or when I was a courier, that was just a job. I didn't feel bad about doing those things, but being a pro skateboarder was something to be proud of. And every time I was reminded that I was a pro skateboarder, it made me feel a little proud all over again. It still does. It's the gift that keeps on giving.

Let me remind everyone reading this book: You are going to die. And you don't get to say when. Death could come knocking at any time. I've always tried to live my life to the fullest. At times I've even been a little over-the-top about that. But when my father and my brother died, a few years back, I took things to yet another level. Now that I had seen death, it made me think that I was going to be next. Death could come sooner than I think.

That mind-set made me want to do everything. It made me think, "If I could get so much satisfaction out of skating, then what else can I do? What can I get out of radio? What can I get out of fighting?" There are so many other facets of life. Before, I might have decided that I'm too busy to fit a bunch of new shit into my life. But now, I am on a perpetual quest.

And it's not for anybody else. It's for my own personal satisfaction. I think if you have that mind-set, that you could die any day— and if you can live with that knowledge in your head without having to take anxiety pills—then that's a productive way to look at things.

Because it makes you fucking hustle.

Here is the bottom line: The Man wants you to be fat and weak, and get a side part in your hair, and eat McDonald's, and play Xbox, and convince yourself you give a shit about Ryan Seacrest and the Real Housewives. The Man wants you to take pills, pay taxes, smoke cigarettes, and die. Those are the facts.

But I'm living proof that it doesn't have to be like that. You don't need to be special to become awesome. You just need to do the work. I learned to spell from Twitter. I still haven't read my last book, and yet I'm a bestselling author. So yes, it can happen to you, too!

There's so much more out there, waiting for you to reach out and take it.

Let me remind you one last time: You are going to die. Guaranteed. And it might not happen when you're old and shriveled up and useless. It could happen today. You could drop dead while you read this sentence. You could get plowed over by a truck. You know this. Everyone knows it. So why don't you act like it? If you just want to cruise through life, you can probably pull it off. But when all is said and done, what will you have to show for yourself?

Getting what you want out of life is your choice. You can cry, and never get laid, and become a useless prick who hates everything. But that's your decision. It's impossible for someone else to give you a bad attitude. Only you can give yourself a bad attitude. You have the power to decide whether or not you give a shit about what other people have to say about you. If you suck, that's your problem. That's your fault.

If you dedicate yourself to being awesome, maybe you won't reach your ultimate goal. But even sucky lives can have windows of glory. Isn't that better than no glory at all?

At times, becoming awesome may be painful. But as they say, pain is just weakness leaving the body. Harden the fuck up.

You may lose focus from time to time. I bet even porn stars get bored of dicks sometimes. But you can't let that stop you. You need to dig deep. You need to plow through your life like a relentless wildebeest.

You need to accept the fact that there is no such thing as trying. Saying that you're trying may not sound like a negative attitude, but it is. You need to believe. You're not trying to be the best. You *will* be the best.

I can move boulders with my mind. I tell myself I am a warlord. I am the fucking best. I am the champion of the world. I make my own world up, and then I make it come true. I guarantee that you can do the same thing.

It's every man for himself. So ask yourself, what do you truly want?

Here's what I want: I want to have it all. I want to be famous. I want to be on TV. I want women to like me and I want dudes to think I'm cool. And then after I have that, I want to leave and go to the bush, and I want to hunt deer and smoke weed. That's the plan. That's what I envision. Me with a big old beard and a bunch of dead animals hanging off my jacket. And my chick is still hot, because she's ten years younger than me. That's where I'm going.

So where are you going? What do you want for your life? And how are you going to get it?

Figure that out. And then follow me to gloryville.

ACKNOWLEDGMENTS

DEVIN AND TIGER ELLIS, Katie Gilbert, Michael Tully, Mark Chait, Bethany Larson, Michael Barrs, Benji Madden, Joel Madden, Dr. Crausman, Will Pendarvis, Josh Richmond, SiriusXM, Tony Hawk, Grant Cobb, Fifty, Burger, Prince, Caino, Supercross the Dragon, Rob Dyrdek, Dingo, Death! Death! Die!, Rob "Sluggo" Boyce, the Red Dragons, Carey Hart, Ricky Carmichael, Chad Reed, Rob Garcia, Juliet Lowrie, Mike Blabac, Jody Morris, Jayson Steele Fox, Donald Schultz, Ryan Steely, Justin Dawes, Rick Kosick, Jeff Tremaine, the Jingleberries, Metallica, Sharks, skateboarding, motocross, Lethal Lee Ellis and his family, Stevie Ellis, the ocean, and the blue sky.

ABOUT THE AUTHORS

JASON ELLIS lives in Los Angeles, where he continues to kick ass on a daily basis. He is the host of SiriusXM's *The Jason Ellis Show*.

MIKE TULLY can be heard daily on *The Jason Ellis Show*.

ALSO BY JASON ELLIS
WITH MIKE TULLY

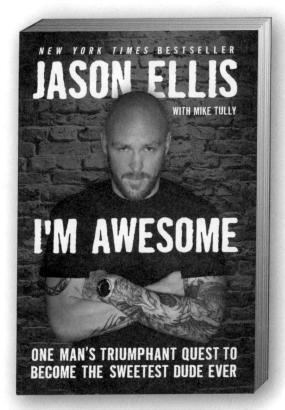

I'M AWESOME
One Man's Triumphant Quest to Become the Sweetest Dude Ever
Available in Paperback and eBook

X Games skateboarder, pro mixed martial arts fighter, and outspoken SiriusXM satellite radio host Jason Ellis shares his jaw-dropping and inspirational life story—from the depths of addiction, to the glory of victory, to the joys and ordeals of fatherhood. Fans of *The Jason Ellis Show* and the MMA-meets-music festival "Ellismania" know Ellis as a fearless daredevil— and as the new voice of action sports in America. Now, fans can learn how he got to be the man he is: the struggles, the setbacks, and the fight he put up to make it through to something better. Fans of Forrest Griffin's *Got Fight?* and Tony Hawk's *Hawk* won't want to miss this unbelievable tell-all from a larger-than-life icon, and a fighter through and through.